SOME THINGS
NEVER CHANGE

Richard Law, Sr.

ISBN: 978-1535204026

THROUGH MY MEMOIR, *Some Things Never Change* I expressed the misery, hatred, and torment I experienced while residing in the bloody Toombs of Lyons and Vidalia, Georgia. That's what Toombs County was called years ago. On May 14, 2016, my son was murdered and buried in Toombs County. It is in his memory that I dedicate my memoir. This book is dedicated to the life of my twenty-nine-year-old son, James Richard Law.

I am saddened with grief because the streets of Vidalia, Georgia have ended the life of my youngest son who, from the very beginning, never had a chance. He was a young man who got caught up in the prison system at a very early age and he was never afforded an opportunity to get it right; not from the day he set foot in the courtroom of Toombs County.

I sat in the courtroom waiting patiently for my son's case to be called. Case after case was called and finally I heard his name. I felt pretty good because I had just heard a case that was similar to what James was being charged with. Needless to say, some things never change. The case I heard was that of a young white boy around James' age; he received only probation. Unfortunately, James got five years. I never understood why James went to jail instead of getting probation. I learned later on that it was because he would not tell on the other boys who had been involved in the crime. He didn't do well in jail because he constantly got into trouble. Most of the time it was a fight with someone or he got caught using a cell phone. It was always something that caused him to miss probation. When he finally came home to Vidalia after five years, he wasn't home for long; it's difficult for an ex-con to get a decent job. This time, he went away for ten years. James was finally released in July of 2015 and met his unfortunate death in May of 2016. In July, he would have been home from prison for one year. I knew in my heart that if James continued to stay in Toombs County, no good would come from it. I constantly encouraged him to come to Savannah and on Mother's Day, he called Johnnie Mae to wish her a Happy Mother's Day. He reported with great joy and enthusiasm that he had an interview for a job at a plant in Pooler on May 24th. Sadly, early in the morning on May 14th, we got a call that James was dead. He never made it to that interview. This book is dedicated to his memory.

In Loving Memory

of

Mr. James Richard Law

Sunrise	Sunset
November 13, 1986	*May 9, 2016*

CONTENTS

FOREWORD

RICHARD LAW, SR., the author of this informative and inspiring memoir, is my husband. No one could have told me that one day I would write the foreword to the story Richard had the courage to tell.

I worked nearly 34 years for the Postal Service where I served in many capacities. At different times, I was a Clerk, Superintendent of Window Services, Accountable Paper Custodian (where I was responsible for stamp stock worth millions of dollars), Retail Supervisor, and, on two occasions, served as Officer-in-Charge (or the Postmaster in Varnville, S. C. and Hardeeville, S.C.). During my time with the postal service, I saw many changes – particularly technical ones – to make the service better for employees and customers. However, I also saw many things that didn't change. Specifically, I was the victim of racism and sexual harassment. I know that I should have moved further up the ladder in the Postal Service, but I was outspoken and vocal, and unfortunately, that served as a hindrance for me. I'm reminded of a white manager who tried to put his tongue in my mouth while suggesting that if I wanted to move up, submitting to his advances was the route I would have to take. I gave him a piece of my mind and I never advanced any further than a supervisor, which, in my opinion, was the Postal Service's loss.

As a result of all I've been through in my own life, I am in support of my husband's belief that some things will never change. I would imagine that many people have untold stories about discrimination against black men and women. All we have to do is look over our lives and compare where we are to the stances some folks still have on certain issues. We'll realize quickly that racism still exists, and it's not hard to find. A large part of our world today is still stuck and isn't moving beyond racism and hatred.

While attending a graduation ceremony at the Savannah Civic Center in 1993, I caught a glimpse of an old friend. I thought to myself, "That is Ricky Law and it has been quite a few years since our paths have crossed." Walking alone and trying my best to be polite, as Ricky stood with a group of people, I did not stop to speak. As I began to reminisce about this man from my past, I gave him a coy smile and thought about our past intimate relationship. He smiled back as though he wanted me to stop and chat, but since I didn't know if he had remarried or was involved with someone, I continued on my way.

A year later destiny allowed us to reunite once again. From the choir stand in church, I looked out into the audience and saw that same familiar face. I saw Ricky Law standing in the midst of the congregation, boldly praising God. I was shocked. Certainly this couldn't be the same person I used to know. I could feel an anointing of brightness through every clap of his hand, which exemplified his love for God. I was overjoyed and surprised to see him in church that day and after the service, I rushed over to embrace him and told him how glad I was to see him. We talked for a few minutes and I remember saying, "Why don't you give me a call?" Without missing a beat, he said, "Let me give you my number and you call me some time." I learned later that he felt the need to have me reach out to him because for years I had rejected him and he had moved on from chasing women.

From that day forward, we rekindled our friendship. Through our many conversations, I learned how the folks in Toombs County had retaliated against Ricky after he filed an EEO complaint. Toombs County refused to compensate him even though the doctors determined he was disabled and it was documented he was unable to perform his work duties. My husband endured a stroke brought on by his employer. Sadly, everyone, including his attorney, turned their back on him. Prior to our marriage, I tried very hard to help him receive the money that was rightfully his, to no avail. However, we were instrumental in causing Toombs County to rewrite the adoption agreement for the Toombs County Pension Fund.

Over and over, Ricky has said that he wanted to tell his story so that he might help just one other person. In his memoir, he tells of his early years when he abused drugs and alcohol. He writes honestly about his marriages and involvement with many women, but God changed him and gave him a charge to keep. I learned quickly that Ricky was a giving man with a huge heart when I witnessed him making financial contributions to people he did not know who had experienced some sort of loss. I thought to myself, "I like this man." The first time I said to him, "I think I love you," he responded, "Love God first." I knew then that he was the man God had chosen for me.

As for me, I've had many storms in my life and I believe that through my husband, God is teaching me that for every trial we endure, there is an expiration date. It is my prayer that God will use Ricky and his story to help you as you move forward in this life with whatever you may encounter.

—*Johnnie Mae Law*

INTRODUCTION

THE YEAR WAS 2006. I sat relaxing in my recliner in the den leisurely browsing through the newspaper with an ear tuned to the radio news broadcast on WTOC. My attention was grabbed when I scanned the page of the *Savannah Morning News* and saw an article mentioning that Toombs County High School seniors were getting ready for their prom. I shook my head ruefully and thought to myself, *Some things in the world will never change.* Just like the saying goes, the more things change, the more they stay the same. We know that whatever is to be has already been, and what will be has been before. God will call the past into account.

I read further into the story and saw that in Lyons, Georgia, in Toombs County, where I had lived for more than twelve years, the prom is different than in many other places in the country. The prom in Lyons is actually two proms: a white prom and a black prom. And now, an entire generation after the Supreme Court declared segregation illegal, a third group of students is pushing for a third, Hispanic prom. I shook my head and asked myself, *What is this world coming to?* Young people, the future of our country, cannot come together under one roof to celebrate that high school rite of passage, the prom. Instead, they must choose between three proms.

Ever since the early 1970s, the idea of separate black and white proms has been a tradition in Toombs County. In an effort to defend the students in the school district and to protect their rights, the school superintendent claims that it is up to each student to decide whom they want to socialize with and which prom he or she wishes to attend. The superintendent added, "People go out to various restaurants, and they like particular things when they get there. That's the way it is with kids. They pick and choose where they want to go and whom they want to party with."

This sounds familiar to me, familiar and old-fashioned. I was reminded of the expression, "Birds of a feather flock together." To me, that has always seemed like an excuse for people to remain insular, segregated, and cut off from experiences and people who may add a great deal to one's life. I don't understand the concept of three separate proms. I think that instead, the young people in Vidalia should grow up and embrace the differences of those around them. Only by doing so can they become the people God has called them to be. Love one another, for love is from God, and whoever loves has been born of God and knows God. You can't love one another if you're holding each other at arm's length.

I have noticed this troubling trend in other instances as well, not just the prom. In an effort to support my nephew John, I attended several of his high school football games. John graduated from a well-known private military school in Savannah and was one of the star players and captain of the team. At his games, I watched anxiously as John ran with the ball, getting closer and closer to the end zone. John ran the ball 65 yards and found himself a few feet from scoring a touchdown. Instead, the coach instructed the quarterback to pass the ball to a white player on the next play. He—and not John—got credit for the touchdown. The first time I saw it, I didn't think much of it, assuming that the coach had his reasons. But then, as I attended more and more games, I saw the same scenario played out again and again. I started to wonder, *Why was the coach allowing the white boys to score a touchdown and take the credit that rightfully should have gone to John?*

Other relatives and parents at the game began noticing what was happening as well and we started to talk about it. I don't remember who first used the word "racism," but it became clear that that's what we were talking about. John's school is predominately white; there are very few black students. The discrepancy in the way the black students were treated was obvious. Some of the parents of the black students claimed that the school was engaging in unfair treatment. "They use our boys to win sports and they never support them as they do the white boys," one parent claimed.

Eventually, I learned that several of the white players had been given full scholarships to attend the private school, while John had only received a partial scholarship. There was no reason for this; his talent is clear and he works as hard as anyone. Things like this make me look around and realize that even though we have supposedly gotten past the hurdle of prejudice—people like to say we live in a "postracial" America—some things remain the same as ever. Over and over again, the same things keep happening.

I set the newspaper aside and my mind wandered. I thought of people like Joe Louis and Jackie Robinson. In their heyday, they were celebrated for breaking down racial barriers. And while they were un-doubtedly talented and did many great things to further the cause of integration, racism clearly still exists. I considered the election of Barack Obama, the first black president, and asked myself, *Have we finally gone beyond racism?* Many people claimed that once we elected a black president, racism would cease to be an American problem. But as I looked around and thought about separate proms and favoritism to white football players, I realized, we have so much further to go.

For the first time in history, the president of the United States of America is an African American. And yet, for all the strides and progress we have made as a country, we have that much further to go. When Obama was elected in 2008, we did not cease to be a racist country overnight; the hatred and racism did not stop. In some cases, the divide grew even greater. While many Republican leaders in Congress would claim that they oppose President Obama's policies and not his race, it's worth noting that no other Democratic president has faced such steadfast Republican opposition from Congress.

The incidents that indicate we are nowhere close to being free of racism seem to happen every day. Don Sterling, former owner of the NBA's Los Angeles Clippers, made racist comments about his girlfriend bringing African Americans to games, claiming that he did not want to be associated with them. These comments were made in 2014, not 1964. Maybe we haven't come as far we thought. Sterling, like many others, comes from an older generation taught to hate those who don't look like them.

Another incident occurred just a couple of years ago when I was visiting family in Brooklyn. The news broke concerning Paula Deen, a popular Food Network star who lives in my hometown. Suddenly, Deen found herself over the media facing allegations that she used the N-word and fantasized about giving her son a plantation-style wedding. She was quoted as saying she would hire an all-black staff to serve her white guests. Deen, like Sterling, is the kind of person who will smile in your face but say negative and hurtful things about you behind closed doors. Their hatred inspires racist comments, but I believe that their evil intentions will be exposed when God shines a light on them.

While many people were outraged at what they perceived as her overt racism, I was not at all surprised. Even though it's kept quiet, Savannah still practices segregation. There are a number of all-white private clubs that do not allow black members. In 2016, these kinds of places still exist. Some things really do never change.

In the state of South Carolina, the murder of a black pastor and eight black church members by a white gunman who allegedly expressed racist sentiments caused a national discussion about whether or not flying the Confederate flag over the state capital sent a message of bigotry and hatred. Finally, Governor Nikki Haley called on the state legislature to immediately begin a process to remove the flag from the statehouse. In July, the Senate voted 37–3 to remove the flag.

President Obama gave a eulogy for Pastor Pinckney, the pastor killed in the Emanuel African Methodist Episcopal Church shooting. He said, "Removing the flag from this state's capitol would not be an act of political correctness; it would not be an insult to the valor of Confederate soldiers. It would simply be an acknowledgment that the cause for which they fought—the cause of slavery—was wrong. The imposition of Jim Crow after the Civil War, the resistance to civil rights for all people, was wrong." The president continued, "It would be one step in an honest accounting of America's history, a modest but meaningful balm for so many unhealed wounds."

And while removing the flag from the statehouse was an important step, months later, many in the community still feel as though they are not allowed to heal. Everywhere you look, there are some people still proudly displaying the Confederate flag. I noticed it myself when we traveled the back roads to watch my grandson, Jalen, play soccer in Warner Robbins, Georgia. Many homes continued to fly confederate flags. On the way, we were even delayed by a parade in Reidsville, Georgia, in which men marched in front of the city's court-house with the same flag that has caused so much pain and suffering.

And so, as I consider the events of my past and the experiences of my life, I realize how far we have come and how much further we have yet to go. My own story is far from simple, as I struggled with drugs, alcohol, and many women in my life. My greatest battle transpired in 1994 when my doctor concluded that I had suffered a stroke. I maintain that the stroke was caused by abuse, discrimination, and racism, all of which I endured while I was employed by Toombs County. I'm grateful that this sickness did not kill me or transform my physical appearance. Only my speech was affected, but for more than a year I was unable to speak. I could understand when people spoke to me, but I could not speak in reply. I knew, for example, that a fork was a fork but I could not say, "That's a fork." The word of God, physical therapy, patience, and perseverance contributed to my ability to pronounce words again. I am saddened by the treatment I received from the folks in Toombs County, and it is my hope and prayer that I can help others who may have had experiences similar to what I went through. Don't get me wrong; not everyone in Toombs County is a bad person. There are a few good folks. But there are also some outright cowards who demonstrate that racism is common and acceptable. They are concealed by those who assert, "I'm not a racist."

I am extremely grateful to the men and women who have sacrificed so much to the cause of overcoming racism, but I contend that some things in this world will never change until we as a people can see each other as people whom God has created equal. Yes, we have made progress, but there is still a long way to go.

CHAPTER 1

AS I SIT HERE REMINISCING about this world, my place in it, and all I've had to endure in my lifetime, I just shake my head in sorrow as I realize that some things will never change. My memories go all the way back to 1964 in Savannah, where I grew up. We lived in a section of town called "Ogeecheeton." This community sits to the north at the bottom of an overpass on Highway 17, often referred to as Ogeechee Road. The location is south of the Cloverdale subdivision and west of Stiles Avenue. It's somewhat hidden because if you're not familiar with the city, you could very easily pass it by.

Richard "Ricky" Law, Sr.

There's a joke among some folks that this small portion of the city is the best-kept secret in Savannah. In this neighborhood, most of the residents are family or lifelong residents. People don't really leave this community either. I remember Mrs. Doe, who lived to be 115 years of age. She spent the majority of her life in the same spot. Then there was my paternal grandmother, Julia Eloise Law, who was 103 when she died. She was a lifer in the neighborhood too. People often joke that the key to their longevity can be found in the drinking water. But for many years, we only had well water because the city didn't bring running water to our community until the early 1970s. Instead, my father, John Law, Sr., kept his well active and we drank from it often. So maybe there is something to the saying that there's something in the water.

My father was employed by the Savannah Coca-Cola Company for over 50 years. He was nearly 90 when he went home to be with the Lord in December of 2006.

My mother Dorothy Law worked hard doing what was then called "domestic work" for a number of years until she was blessed to get a job at St. Joseph/Candler Hospital, formerly Candler/Telfair Hospital. She retired in March of 1991 after spending 22 years working as a surgical tech aide. Mom was always telling us about the packets of linen she had to prepare for daily use prior to a person having surgery. She said after the linen was packed it was them sent for sterilization before it was used.

Mom & Dad: Dorothy and John Law, Sr.

I was just 13 years old myself when I got my very first job at the Blue Top Motel on Highway 17. I was so excited about working because I knew I would have money in my pockets to buy my own clothes and the All-Star high-top sneakers all the boys were wearing. I enjoyed the latest rock and roll music, so I bought all the latest LPs and 45 rpm records. Sometimes, on special occasions I would purchase gifts for my parents like the cartons of cigarettes I bought them for Christmas. This remains something I regret to this day because of all the complications tobacco has caused my mother. Though she is 90 years young, she has to use oxygen and a walker every day.

The Blue Top Motel consisted of cabins made of brick. The ground on which the motel sat was nothing but dirt covered over with roofing shingles. Part of my job was to escort guests to their cabins. As I led them across the shingled ground, key in my hand, I would smile from ear to ear. I loved the responsibility and the fact that I was working and earning money on my own. I truly enjoyed the job because every now and then, someone would bless me with a really nice tip. I learned early on that the bigger the smile, the greater the chance at a nice tip.

Unfortunately, I didn't work at the Blue Top for very long, because Bobby, the motel manager, was an ex-prizefighter who often got drunk and liked to pretend he could still fight. He'd fixate on me and challenge me to fight him. I can still clearly recall several instances when he would bully me with his fists. After a while, no matter how good the tips were, that kind of thing wears on you. So it wasn't long before I began to look for another job.

It didn't take me too long to find one. My brother Jimmy worked at the Exxon station a bit further down Ogeechee Road, and I got a job at the Chevron station right across the street.

At the time, Ogeechee Road—or Highway 17—was a busy access road. My job was to pump gas, check the oil, check the tires, and clean the restrooms of the gas stations as cars whizzed by on the street. As I think back on that job and all the people I came into contact with while working at the Chevron station, I realize that I don't remember many black people stopping to purchase gas or have their oil changed. I don't really know why that was, but it's the truth.

Mr. Dan, the station's owner, allowed me to work at least five days a week, giving me one day off during the middle of the week. The station was closed on Sundays, but during the week he would often pick me up for work and drive me home at night.

Jimmy and Ricky Law

Mr. Dan hired two other black men, Kevin and Jack, to work as mechanics around the shop. My interaction with these men was very limited. Perhaps it was because I was just a 13-year-old kid and we didn't have much of anything in common.

Kevin was out on parole for murder but had been vouched for by Mr. Dan, a member of the parole board. He was in a position to help men just getting out of prison and I imagine that he was trying to give Kevin a new start in life by giving him a job and watching over him. I spoke to Kevin and Jack when I could but our conversations were limited. Nevertheless, certain memories stand out in my mind. In particular, I remember them telling me about the small hole in the ladies' bathroom that Kevin and Jack often used to peep at the women who visited the station.

It might have been all the whiskey they drank while working that caused them to participate in such unethical acts. It wasn't exactly diffi-cult for them to get the booze, since the package store was located right next door to the Chevron station. They certainly had the opportunity.

It wasn't long before Kevin returned to prison again. He was convicted of murder, the same crime he'd been committed for the first time around.

By now Mr. Dan was getting older, and he decided it was time to retire. He sold the gas station to his competitor Mr. Jack, who decided to keep me on his payroll, which helped me out a lot. I didn't have to find a new job.

About nine months after Mr. Jack bought the station, he too decided to sell. Thankfully, he owned another business located just a bit further down Highway 17. He must have appreciated my work ethic because he kept me on as an employee and I still had a job.

This location was more than just a gas station. It consisted of a trailer park with a service station and a tackle shop. It was a very busy spot because the shop also sold boats and camper trailers. I was always busy and worked at this location under Mr. Jack for almost three years.

Sometimes Mr. Jack would give me a ride home after work, but I usually walked. It was a good little hike—probably less than three miles—and a good opportunity to stretch my legs after a day at work. But on the nights Mr. Jack gave me a ride home, he would stop by the liquor store to purchase a bottle of whiskey on the way. He thought nothing of sending me into the store to buy his whiskey for him even though I was only about 14. Back then no one thought twice of selling whiskey to a teenager.

For many years the sale of alcoholic beverages in the state of Georgia was prohibited on Sundays. However, that didn't stop Mr. Jack from selling beer to certain people on Sunday. His business was close to a racetrack where folks gathered on the weekends for fun and games. Somebody was always looking to purchase beer on Sunday and needed somewhere to buy it.

The word must have gotten out that Mr. Jack had beer for sale because he sold more beer on Sunday from his service station than he sold during the week!

It seemed as though Mr. Jack knew everyone, including the chief of the Sheriff's Department, who owned and operated a popular fishing camp in town. Even the chief was a frequent Sunday beer customer, despite the prohibition. Whenever Mr. Jack saw the chief drive up, he would put two six-packs in a large bag and walk it outside to the chief's car personally.

During this time, the Vietnam War was happening and soldiers were frequently returning home from the war. One day, two soldiers came into the station with their wives looking to rent a trailer. One couple was white and the other was black. I don't recall exactly what was said but I remember that Mr. Jack refused to rent them a trailer because he didn't rent to blacks; his trailer park was "whites only."

When the two families left the shop, Mr. Jack immediately got on the telephone to call up some of his buddies to tell them about the incident and how he handled it. He boasted about how he'd stood up to them and put his foot down. He was proud of what he'd done.

Later that evening, one of Mr. Jack's friends stopped by the station. Quickly, he shooed me and another black coworker away, as though he didn't want us near him. I should have been a fly on the wall because I'm sure they had a wonderful time discussing what had just transpired.

This was my first real encounter with racism. I found myself agitated and angry. It didn't feel right and I knew what Mr. Jack was doing wasn't right. I wanted to do something to pay him back for the racist attitude he had for God's people. I had no shortage of devious evil thoughts and ideas about what I could do, but then I realized that I was just a young black boy with little power. Nevertheless, I couldn't get the idea of revenge out of my head.

I spoke about my feelings to my coworker and he agreed that we needed to make Mr. Jack pay. The following Saturday at work we decided that when it was time for us to empty the trash, we would mysteriously disappear. In other words, we got "lost" and Mr. Jack was stuck doing all the work including pumping gas. A bit later on, we decided we had better get back to work, but I had no idea what was in store for me. Mr. Jack allowed us to work for a short while before approaching the both of us, turning to me and saying, "I no longer need your help." He fired me, paid me, and sent me on my way. Our plan had backfired. Nevertheless, I thanked him and decided that since I had newfound free time, I would visit my sister, Dorothy Deshazior, in Miami.

CHAPTER 2

THE SUMMER BEFORE I was set to enter 11th grade, I spent my entire summer vacation in Miami. My sister worked on Miami Beach at Mount Sinai Hospital and I was fortunate enough to get a summer job there. I was responsible for delivering milk, juice, and cookies to the nurse's station while the nurses delivered the food to the patients. I loved this job because it made me feel really grown-up and responsible, working with so many important people like nurses and doctors.

One day, my sister and I were in the hospital cafeteria having lunch when a young black physician approached our table and introduced himself. During the conversation he gave me his address and suggested I stop by some time.

I realized that he didn't live too far from my sister, so the next time I had a day off, I decided to take him up on his invitation. He lived in a very nice area of Miami and he was married to a very good-looking woman who arrived home just before I left. During my visit, I kept getting the strangest feeling about this doctor because he seemed to be hinting that he was interested in me. I wasn't sure what to make of it other than to decide it was time for me to leave. I thought he was someone I could look up to because he was a doctor. I thought he would encourage me or be someone who might be interested in mentoring me. This taught me to be very cautious about people and certain situations I might encounter.

I met a lot of people that summer. One man in particular stands out. He worked at the grocery store across the street from my sister's house. He was very friendly and he lived in a section of Miami called Liberty City. We became friendly and began to talk more, and as we talked, it wasn't long before we discovered that he knew all of my cousins, my Uncle Bubba's children. He said, "I know Angela, Beverly, Linda, Charlesetta, Barbara Jean, Gregory, and Anthony!" It wasn't long before I started hanging out with him and some of his friends pretty regularly. We would go to Orange Bowl stadium every Friday because back then the Miami Dolphins had a winning team coached by Don Shula. I remember going to a game between the Chicago Bears and the Miami Dolphins. I believe this was the year Bob Griese was playing quarterback for Miami. Also playing for Miami were Mark Clayton, Mark Duper, Paul Warfield, Larry Csonka, Larry Little, Mercury Morris, and Joe Rose. Gale Sayers was the running back for the Chicago Bears.

Richard and Uncle Willie Echols (Blackie)

Miami was famous for its dog-track gambling, and my uncle (now deceased), whom we lovingly called Blackie, gave me my very first exposure to betting at the dog track. It was interesting and fun to watch dogs chasing a rabbit around the track. People attending the dog-track races would make bets on their favorite dog before the race began. The dog that ran the fastest would be the winner. Winning was both good and bad because sometimes I would win, and then I would bet my winnings only to lose the money I had just won. Blackie was married to my mother's sister, Betty Ann, and he was a great guy and a lot of fun to be around.

By the end of the summer, I was in love with Miami and I wanted to stay, but my mother convinced me that I should come home to Georgia to finish school.

During my high school days, I worked after school at the Trade Wind Shrimp Factory in Thunderbolt, Georgia. Thunderbolt is a small town located in Chatham County about five miles southeast of Savannah. I was enrolled in a program at school called Diversified Career Technology, so I got out of school each day around 12:00 p.m. The program was designed so that students could leave school early to work at a job. Many days I would walk or catch the city bus to Thunderbolt. Trade Wind Shrimp also hired and provided transportation to many of the black women who worked for them. The company had several buses that picked up employees in various low-income areas of the city. When these women would arrive at the factory, they would bread the shrimp. My job was to clean the rooms that were used to weigh shrimp. There were many times when I'd find stray shrimp on the floor and I'd take them home. On those days, we'd have shrimp for dinner! Though I spent most of my time cleaning the shrimp-weighing rooms, I was occasionally allowed to work on the docks unloading shrimp from the boats. That was heavy work.

Although I worked every day, I had plenty of time to hang out with the guys on the docks. They were much older than me because I was still in high school. Every Thursday and Friday evening we'd go out drinking to a little bar called Gus's. This turned out to be the beginning of my drinking career. I didn't know it at the time, but I was about to start a period of my life when I would do a whole lot of drinking and a whole lot of getting drunk at a very young age.

Before I began the 12th grade, I got a summer job at Union Camp, which, after a merger in 1999 became the home of International Paper. When I worked there, it was the largest paper mill in the South. Because the company was so large, it had a major impact on Savannah politics. But it was also highly respected because it kept Savannah from feeling many of the brutal effects of the Great Depression. Many black men were hired by Union Camp, and the company paid well, particularly for men trying to provide for their families.

Beyond the fair pay and the economic help, Union Camp was known for the smell it released into the air. The small of rotten eggs spread out for miles around Union Camp. The stench was so strong that you could smell the plant before you saw it. There was no mistaking that smell.

My job was to pick up the excess paper that fell to the floor under the paper machine. At the plant, this kind of work was done almost predominantly by blacks, as segregation was on the rise. At lunchtime, the black employees we were only allowed to purchase food through a small window, similar to the take-out windows at fast food restaurants today. We were not allowed to sit and eat in the cafeteria with the rest of the workers. The cafeteria was whites only. Of course the restrooms were also separate, and the ones that were provided for the black workers were tiny, really no bigger than a walk-in closet.

In contrast, the white workers had a huge restroom. They all worked the machine jobs, which were not as physically taxing, while the black workers held all the jobs requiring manual labor.

There were only a few black women. You could probably count them on your fingers. I was told by Brenda Lee, a woman who was hired in 1967 by Union Camp through the unemployment office, that the person who conducted her interview told her that the starting salary was $2.67 an hour. Her interviewer called the Union Camp office to describe Brenda and said she was "a very attractive young lady."

Brenda was hired and a white female worker was assigned to train her. The woman showed Brenda around and said to her, "You're the first colored girl to touch these machines." She went on to say that the government was the reason the company was hiring black workers and that if the company didn't comply, the government would shut them down. At first, Brenda was frightened hearing these kinds of things, but she hung in there, put her head down, and went to work. Because of Brenda's light complexion, white employees often asked her if she was of mixed race. Brenda would always reply, "I'm colored, that's all I know." After she saw the other black women who worked the other shifts, Brenda realized that the lighter your skin, the longer your hair, and the "whiter" your features, the easier it was to get by in the company.

Harvey Kennedy was a great guy and a good friend of mine who also worked for Union Camp at the same time as I was employed there. He reminded me of some of the hardships that black men like us had to endure in the workplace. Things like emptying the trash, which were tasks only assigned to black employees, were something we had to deal with. It was often a struggle. When you were dumping the trash cans, you weren't allowed to walk between the machines, so something that should have been easy became more difficult. We were required to stand at one end of the machine while a white employee passed the trash basket to us. They did this so that we wouldn't get too close to the white women who were working there. This was racism, for sure, but it didn't bother me that much at the time because I was so grateful to have gotten the job. I was satisfied with the amount of money I was being paid, which was about $2.90 an hour. Considering that I was still in high school, I was pleased with my situation.

In 1972, I graduated from Alfred E. Beach High School and went back to work at Union Camp. This time I was assigned to the pulp mill and the section of the factory that housed the tanks that needed to be dumped. The tanks were filled with chemicals and chipped wood that was used in the production of paper. Whenever I worked with the tanks, I had to wash them out with a large hose, much like the kind a fireman would use. Every time I used the large hose, I felt like an accident was just waiting to happen. Sure enough, one day it did. At work one day, while washing a tank filled with chemicals I got burned near my crotch area on both thighs. The burns were so severe that I was forced to see my physician, Dr. Henry Collier, the next day.

Dr. Collier told me that I had second-degree burns. He gave me a shot, wrote me a note, and sent me back to work. I took the note to the head superintendent at the factory, who angrily told me that I should have gone to see the company doctor before going to my own physician. According to him, that was the proper protocol. However, when I woke up the next morning and saw the damage to my skin, all I could think was that I needed help immediately.

Shortly after my accident, the company began to lay off workers. Soon, I found myself without work for nearly six weeks before the factory called me back. When they did, I was assigned to the bag factory, the department responsible for making brown paper bags. These were the same brown paper bags that every store used. But in the 1970s, retailers began replacing paper bags with the less expensive plastic shopping bags. Until recently with the increased attention on "green" consumer practices, we still didn't see many paper shopping bags.

CHAPTER 3

BY NOW I FELT as though I was on top of the world! I was having a ball. Back in the day we would often say, "I feel as though I owned all the cotton in Augusta!" I was working, making money, drinking, hanging out with my friends, and attending concerts at the Savannah Civic Center. I enjoyed performances by artists like the Supremes, the Commodores, the O'Jays, and the Jackson Five. Much of my leisure time was spent on the east side of town in a housing project known as Hitch Village. It was there that I met Elmira, who would later become my wife and the mother of my first child, Richard Law, Jr. My marriage to Elmira was very short; I don't believe we were married even a full year. We got married because Elmira was pregnant and it was what many people insisted was "the right thing to do." It's what you did back then if you found yourself in that situation. So we got married. At 19, I was still very immature; just a baby myself. I was too young and Lord knows I was not prepared for marriage, much less ready to be a father. But we seemed to have no choice in the matter. It didn't take long for me to feel like my youth had been cut short, that I hadn't been able to have all the fun I wanted—hadn't been able to live it up. Shortly after Elmira and I got married, I started messing around with other women.

Eventually, I realized that the marriage had been a mistake. So I contacted Clarence Mayfield, a popular black attorney, and filed for a divorce. At the time, I was already involved with Bessie, who would eventually become my second wife and the mother of my second child, Chassidy.

Bessie was extremely nice and good looking. She worked at the pay window of Union Camp and whenever I went to pick up my check, I found myself checking her out. I always greeted her quickly, but on one particular day I decided to be bold and ask her name. "Bessie," she told me and gave me her telephone number.

I started calling her and we began dating. I often took her to the popular nightclubs in Savannah like the Progressive Center, the Elks Club, and the Lion's Den. Back then we enjoyed ourselves and didn't feel so much of the pressure that I feel like young folks today are faced with. Even so, seemingly in the blink of an eye I was married again and had a new baby girl.

After working for a year at Union Camp, I was laid off again. This time I decided that instead of waiting around to see if I would be called back, I would sign up for the Army. The recruiter I met with gave me his approval and I walked out, light as air, thinking I had been accepted into the Army. But for some reason unknown to me I was never admitted into the Army.

Without the Army as an option, I decided to apply for a job with the FBI. But that didn't go as planned either. My life was at a standstill.

Because I was still young and restless, I continued to hang out with my buddies and shirk my responsibilities at home. I wasn't faithful to Bessie, just as I hadn't been to Elmira, because I lacked the knowledge of God's word. I was also drinking an awful lot and a drink was always close to hand. My liquor bottle and I were like two peas in a pod. I would get so drunk that I'd believe I was sober, which would, in turn, cause me to drink even more.

At the time, Bessie and I were living on Bull Street, about three blocks from the Looking Glass Lounge. Back in the day, Bull Street was often called "the strip" and it was a popular hangout location for both young and older adults. As soon as I got off work, I would head straight to the club, where I would stay until closing time. I became addicted to the club life and found myself spending all of my time there; I'd arrive when it opened and leave after it closed. Life was wild and crazy. And even with my tenuous family situation, my increased drinking, my lack of employment, and my womanizing, I continued to feel like I was on top of the world.

Finally, Union Camp called me back to work again. As always, I was still hanging out in the clubs. Every other Friday evening when I got off work I'd head over to Drake and Joel's Barber Shop for a shape-up or to have my Afro trimmed. The shop was located almost directly across from another popular club I loved to frequent called the Oasis Lounge. I'd walk straight out of the barber shop, cross the street, and be in the club in no time.

That Oasis Lounge called to me as though a magnetic force was pulling me in. Sometimes I swore I could hear someone calling my name. "Ricky Law," it would say, "we're waiting on you." I almost never ignored the voice.

There was another spot I liked further down Highway 17 called the Seashell Restaurant. It was one of the original popular spots for young black Vietnam veterans who had returned home to Savannah in the late sixties and early seventies. Right behind the restaurant there were cabins that local men and women seeking privacy could rent. I must admit I was a frequent visitor to this location, particularly because these were grounds close to where I grew up.

CHAPTER 4

MY JOB AS A MACHINE OPERATOR at Union Camp was hard because we were constantly being laid off about every six months. Many of us had to get by on unemployment. It felt like just as soon as were got squared away with the unemployment office to receive benefits, Union Camp would call us back to work again. This went on for more than two years. Personally, I wasn't overly concerned about my work situation because I was young and having the time of my life. Or so I thought.

By now, I had four years seniority working for Union Camp, with two years working in the bag factory, and a lot of the older workers had started to retire. This opened up a window of opportunity for several of us to train as adjusters. All of us were black with the exception of one white guy. Despite the odds being in my favor, the situation didn't work out for me because the person in charge of training us was also white. At the time in Georgia, racism was not hidden; it was out in the open and it was common. The trainer overlooked me and the work I could do and promoted the white employee over me, even though I had seniority over him.

The plant was a hotbed of prejudice and racism. There was only one black foreman, and he was in charge of the "labor gang," a group of employees who were responsible for cleaning, dumping trash, and other jobs requiring manual labor. All of the men who worked under him were also black. Back then, no one could imagine a black man supervising a white worker.

In 1971, a well-known civil rights firebrand black attorney and state legislator named Bobby Hill, along with his white partner Fletcher Farrington from Selma, Alabama, represented several black employees in a discrimination lawsuit against Union Camp. The class action suit was settled out of court and compensation was given to all black workers. After this settlement, doors began to open for black employees, allowing us to move into positions we had never before been allowed to occupy. Many blacks became foremen, pipe fitters, and even welders. We were starting to move into white men's jobs.

Even though things were improving, they were still not perfect. We were still horribly mistreated and many of the older black workers decided to go back to their old jobs. Younger guys like myself stuck it out and tried to hold on. We were often paired with a white employee who was tasked with training us, but during this period, the white guy wouldn't even bother to learn our name.

Through it all my lifestyle remained the same. I still spent my time partying, hanging out, and having a ball. I didn't realize it then but I had developed a serious drinking problem. I began to hang out in different places and with different people.

I began to spend a lot of my leisure time at juke joints. Savannah had a lot of these spots back in the day and they were popular in the black communities. Juke joints were usually ramshackle buildings or private houses that offered food, drink, dancing, and gambling. Some juke joint owners made extra money selling moonshine to patrons or by remaining open all hours of the night. They were generally open on Sundays because the liquor stores were closed and people needed someplace to get their alcohol fix.

Eventually, realizing how much I enjoyed frequenting Savannah's juke joints, I decided to open up a little spot of my own in Liberty City. I was going to be a businessman and run my very own juke joint! Every Friday, Saturday, and Sunday I would open for a crowd who enjoyed eating crabs and drinking beer and wine. We'd have music and dancing as well. Back then Lou Rawls, Marvin Gaye, James Brown, The Supremes, and Aretha Franklin were popular.

This little business of mine allowed me to meet a lot of people from the neighboring counties. A group of friends from nearby Effingham County came in to party and for some reason, they left carpet on the side of my juke joint. I wasn't sure why they left it there but I decided to view it as an opportunity. I tapped into my entrepreneurial spirit.

I was still married to Bessie and she knew some people who were interested in purchasing carpet. She asked me to take the carpet to a woman who lived on Habersham and 32nd Streets. I agreed but had no idea what to expect.

When I arrived, I was surprised to learn that the woman was someone I had been trying unsuccessfully to meet for some time. I was shocked to see that this was the lady I had seen driving that orange Volkswagen Beetle with the Rolls Royce front and back around Savannah. This was the lady I wanted to get to know. As I unloaded the carpet, I racked my brain for a way to strike up a conversation. She began counting out money to pay me and I started to ask her questions. "What's your name?" I asked. "Are you married?" "Where do you hang out?"

She told me she wasn't married and that she worked at the post office. I was trying very hard not to talk too much because I really wanted to get to know her. I looked her up and down and said to myself, "Man!" I was impressed.

After I left, I couldn't stop thinking about her. I started to ask around to see if anyone else knew her. I wasn't able to find out much more, and time passed. I didn't see her for a long time. Bessie and I were struggling in our marriage. We went back and forth between being together and being separated. We spent a lot of time trying to resolve our differences.

Then one night I spotted the woman I had sold the carpet to in a club. As I watched her move around and take a seat between George and LaRue, two letter carriers I knew, I screwed up my courage and self-esteem and approached them. I heard one of them call her by name. "Hey, Johnnie Mae," he said. I stayed back and observed her from afar.

I didn't get to talk with her that night but several weeks later she walked into the joint I was running. Right then and there I made up my mind that I was determined to get to know her. A bit later on, an opportunity presented itself and we talked and talked. We talked and drank for several hours and eventually decided to ride to Hardeeville, South Carolina, 21 miles from Savannah. We went to a club in Hardeeville and sat around drinking beer and shooting pool.

On the way back to Savannah, we decided to stop at a motel, where we spent the night. I thought this was the beginning of our relationship until she told me she was seeing someone. After that night, I would occasionally see her in clubs, but our conversations were always very brief.

Time and time again I found myself visiting many of the nightclubs I thought she went to with the hope of running into her. Every now and then I'd catch a glimpse of her passing through with several of her girlfriends. On several occasions she seemed to be alone, but most of the time she was with her girlfriend Doris McFadden Brown. The two of them never stayed in one place for too long.

One rainy night on Bull Street as I sat in the Scorpio Lounge drinking and talking to a couple of guys, I met Robbie E. Robinson, another popular attorney who challenged racial discrimination. He was a city alderman representing the Fifth District. He was easy to talk to and down to earth. I later learned that he and Johnnie Mae were childhood friends; his mother and her grandmother were close.

We drank and talked about everything from women to politics. Each of us tried to beat the other in paying for the next round of drinks. From that very moment, we were friends. Every now and then we would run into each other; our conversations were mostly about women and racial discrimination. I learned that Robbie was one of the first blacks to attend an all-white school in Savannah. Robbie boasted that he had no fear when he volunteered to cross racial lines at Savannah High School in the early sixties. He was adamant about the civil rights movement and the NAACP. He talked about how he worked in the office with attorney Bobby Hill, who handled the litigation against Union Camp.

Robbie died in 1989 when he was targeted by a mail bomb. His death affected the entire community of Savannah. I learned later that

Robbie and several others were targeted because of their participation in federal litigation involving the NAACP. Racism was alive and well. It might have been decades later, but the mail bomb was the same as the noose that had killed many black men in the past. The more things change, the more they stay the same.

Attorney Robbie Edward Robinson
Courtesy of Ruth Teasley (sister to Robbie)

CHAPTER 5

EVEN THOUGH I WAS INTRIGUED by Johnnie Mae, I continued to see many other women. While most of them were single, quite a few of them were married. Savannah was a popular location with many opportunities for couples who were having an affair and needed a hideaway. One woman I was seeing was a married schoolteacher. One Saturday night we were clubbing at Shavers Lounge on Highway 21. This club was perfect for people who were cheating on their spouses because just behind the club were several motel rooms available for rent.

My friend and I sat and talked and we both ordered wine. After the waiter placed our drinks on the table she got up to use the ladies room. I was feeling sociable so I moved over to a nearby table where some guys I knew from work were sitting. We sat drinking, telling jokes, and trying to impress each other with lies as I waited for my date to return.

As I waited, a man walked through the door and someone at my table looked at me and said, "That's the husband of the woman you're with."

"Better not go back to your table when she comes back!" someone joked, and you better believe I didn't. I spent the rest of the night with the guys I'd befriended. We drove to other clubs and house parties and had a grand old time.

My lady friend left with her husband and called me the next day to tell me that she was pretty sure her husband had been at the motel in the back with another woman himself. Shortly thereafter, this same woman told me that she was pregnant and the baby was mine. When she asked what I thought she should do, I said, "Whatever is best for you." A bit later on, she told me she'd had an abortion. We continued to see each other for a little while longer but before long, the relationship ended.

I still had my job at Union Camp, and one day I was adjusting the paper machines and got my index finger caught in the machine's gears. I couldn't see it myself because another machinist quickly threw a towel over my hand. He rushed me to the infirmary, where the nurse gave me a shot for the pain. An ambulance arrived and I was taken to Candler Hospital, where the emergency room physician immediately took me into surgery.

I remember waking up in the recovery room with my mother standing over me. I looked down at my finger wrapped in gauze and was told that I had lost most of my index finger. After it healed and the bandages were removed, I had only a small piece of my finger left.

At the time, Union Camp did not have any kind of protective covering over the gears of the machine. Shortly after my accident, they installed guards on all the machines. I was out of work for about eight weeks and was receiving worker's compensation. Union Camp instructed me to file a claim with Jones, Hill, and Mercer Insurance Company on Bay Street. I remember signing papers and being given a check for $2,000 for my pain and suffering. Today I realize what a small sum of money that was for losing an entire finger, even in 1979.

The situation didn't curb my drinking at all because I was still drinking and driving. In the early morning as I was leaving what used to be Your House Restaurant on Oglethorpe and MLK Boulevard, I got stopped by the police, who determined that it was necessary to take me to jail. I went to jail that morning and my father paid the bond the next day. My court appearance was in recorder's court, where the presiding judge was Lionel Drew. I was only required to go to DUI School, where I watched a video of accidents caused by drunk drivers. *Sweet,* I thought!

Still wild and foolish a couple of years later, I was stopped again and received my second DUI leaving the same restaurant in the early morning hours. I went to jail again but I was able to post my bond and the courts mandated that I had to pay a fine. Things went well for me for a while until I was leaving my favorite restaurant again and was stopped by the police. It seemed strange to me that I always got stopped after leaving Your House Restaurant. They must have been waiting nearby knowing that's where people were drinking late at night. By now it was obvious; I knew in my heart that I had a problem but I was in denial. This time my court appearance devastated me because it meant I had to go before Judge Drew again. He advised me to find an attorney. Attorney James Bass, who is now a judge, was in court that day and he assisted me.

By the time I received my fourth DUI in Savannah, I remembered attorney James Bass, who had become familiar with me. So before I appeared in court, I went to his office and asked him to represent me. My license was suspended for a year, making me dependent on family, friends, and public transportation.

As time passed, things between Bessie and I didn't work out. Eventually, we got a divorce and I moved back into my parent's home.

At this point I had moved on from alcohol and began experimenting with cocaine. I was quickly becoming a drug addict as well as an alcoholic. After my accident, I worked the day shift for a few months, which worked out great for me. But it wasn't long before Union Camp began to rotate me between the midnight shift and the 3:00 p.m.–11:00 p.m. shift. My drinking began to affect my performance at work and I started having trouble showing up on time. Because of the varied work shifts, I often found myself falling asleep on the job.

According to Harvey Kennedy, I came to work so drunk one day that I managed to crawl underneath one of the machines and fell fast asleep. A young white girl saw me sleeping and thought I was dead so she went running to Harvey. He dragged me to the bathroom and told me to pull myself together. Thank God I had a great supervisor who liked both Harvey and me. He was always looking out for us. Anyone else would have fired me on the spot.

Another time I'm told I was so drunk that I went into the bathroom and fell asleep on the toilet. Harvey said he had to crawl under the door in order to unlatch it and wake me up. Then he went to my boss and asked for me to be relieved of my duties for the day. He assured my boss that he would work extra hard in order to complete his work as well as mine. Harvey was a true friend.

The problems at work weren't the end of my issues. Once I was traveling through Reedsville, Georgia, and got pulled over for drinking and driving. I stayed in jail overnight and my brother John posted bond the next morning. The Lord was still looking out for me because I was only required to pay a fine of $150.

Even though I was still in darkness, I did not realize that the Lord was keeping watch over me. I continued on my destructive path until a couple of years later when I got stopped in Toombs County for drinking and driving again. That time my license was suspended for two years.

One night after finishing my three to seven shift, I decided to stop by a club. My memory surrounding the circumstances of that night are a bit vague but I'm sure I was drunk. I did a whole lot of drinking that night and when I left, I was stopped by the police.

I was unable to provide the officer with my driver's license so I went to jail. The following day I was released on bond and was told to appear in court two weeks later.

Realizing I had made another big mistake, I went to court on the appointed date prepared to face the consequences. I assumed I would be ordered to pay another fine. To my surprise, I was sentenced to serve time. According to my mother, Judge Karp looked over my records and said, "Based on your history of drinking and driving, there is no way you can pay a fine today; you will have to do the time." I was sentenced to eight months in jail, of which I was told I would have to serve half. Things were getting seriously out of control.

CHAPTER 6

WHILE I WAS INCARCERATED, my father's brother T.J. died and my brother Jimmy came home from where he lived in Pompano Beach, Florida, to attend his funeral. Jimmy came to visit me in jail and one of the sergeants on duty told him that I was going to be released shortly. The Lord was still with me because the jail was overcrowded and I was released in less than sixty days, instead of the four months I'd been told I would have to serve.

Sadly, this time my incarceration cost me my job at Union Camp. A bit later I learned that I had been locked up just a bit too long to keep my job. If I had been able to get back to work within a couple of weeks, I wouldn't have been terminated.

Newly unemployed, I decided to go Pompano Beach with my brother Jimmy. I was there for only two weeks when my mom called me and said, "Your attorney has been trying to contact you concerning a case in Toombs County." I realized it must be for that fourth DUI charge from Toombs County. My mom said, "Son, you better make your way back home."

I went to court for a preliminary hearing. I was told I would have to come back later for the actual court case. When I returned, the judge sentenced me to four months in jail and a $750 fine with two years' probation. Just when it seemed like things were looking up, I found myself back in jail.

After I'd been in jail for about two weeks, I had a visitor from the office of Sheriff Charles Durst. A deputy nicknamed Midget came to see me. "The sheriff wants to talk to you," he said. I wondered what in the world the sheriff could possibly want to talk to me about.

Midget was my escort to the sheriff's office, which was only a few feet away. When I arrived at his office, I stood in front of his desk and waited for him to speak. Eventually he said, "Richard, a lot of people like you." I stood still and wondered who he was talking about. The sheriff gave me an ultimatum: "You can stay in Toombs County and work in the shop repairing the county's equipment, or you can go to one of the other work camps." The sheriff looked at me and said, "I'd prefer you stay in Toombs County." The more he talked, the better I enjoyed our conversation.

He said I could work in the shop from Monday through Friday and go home on the weekends. Not wanting to sound too anxious, I told him, "It really doesn't make a difference to me, sir, because either way, I'm required to make the time." With that, the sheriff decided I would stay in Toombs County. I'm still grateful to this day that he made that choice for me.

On Monday morning I reported to work along with a white man from Baxley, Georgia, who also had a DUI charge. That day I met Maxwell Martin, a mechanic who had been employed with the county for a number of years. Back then Toombs County had approximately twenty employees on its payroll. But the man from Baxley and myself were not compensated for our work. Our "compensation" was being able to work in the shop, go home on the weekends, and be on the outside rather than locked up in a jail. We were also given the opportunity to have an additional meal as the other prisoners did not get lunch.

I had no problem whatsoever adjusting to the work that was required of me. After all, I was incarcerated. Just about every day we would leave the shop to work on the county's heavy-duty equipment like the trash trucks, dump trucks, and tractors. I always rode with Mr. Martin, and that pleased me because I could see right away that he was a good person. Being outside on the roads was the highlight of my day.

This job taught me many skills as an auto mechanic that would prove helpful to me later on down the road when I needed to work on my own vehicle. I didn't mind working and I tried to be a good worker, which did not go unnoticed by Mr. Martin.

One afternoon while we were working in the shop, Mr. Martin hollered out to Mel Taylor, chairman of the county commissioners, who came through the shop daily, "Hey, Mel, I got two guys from the jail working over here with me. One's from Baxley, the other is from Savannah, and they do a fine job. You might want to look at hiring these fellows when they get out."

I don't remember exactly what Mr. Taylor said in reply, but later on, after I had been working at the shop for over six weeks, he said to me, "When you get out of jail, we may have to look at keeping you on permanently." He said, "Learn all you can, Richard." I will never forgot that, and I've always tried to follow his advice.

That really made my day. I was truly glad he saw something in me because the truth is, I was really trying to do a good job. As I continued my work, I thought to myself, "It's a real good day." The day got even better when I ran into my attorney, who was on his way to court. He told me the district attorney would be reviewing my case and there was a chance we might go back to court very soon.

Soon after, I went back to court and they released me from jail. It was the best day of my life, although it wasn't long before the realization that I had lost my job at Union Camp began to settle in. I had hoped to one day retire from Union Camp because I'd had myself a really good job. But now my money was short and I wondered how I was going to pay child support and probationary fees to Toombs County. I had the blues.

The next day I reported to work as usual and a week later Mel Taylor advised me to fill out an application for permanent employment. He kept his word and I was hired in the same shop I had been working in while I was incarcerated.

In addition to working for the county, I spent weekends working for Mr. Martin, who had a business servicing wells. His business kept him pretty busy so he hired me to help him out. I worked with him for over 11 years and I enjoyed working with him on both jobs. Mr. Martin was the kind of person who didn't judge you because of the color of your skin but who cared about your abilities and the contents of your heart.

CHAPTER 7

THOUGH I CONTINUED TO DRINK and get drunk, I held on to my job and any additional work that came my way. I did this mainly because I had those probation and child support fees hanging over me. Mel Taylor had a tobacco farm and he offered me work, which I willingly accepted. Many Saturday mornings he would pick me up and I would work the entire day on his tobacco farm harvesting tobacco and preparing it for air curing in a big barn. There were two other black guys who worked with me in the field, and even though the heat was awfully hot none of us seemed to mind. We loaded the tobacco on the truck and transferred it to the barn, where it was cured and prepared for transport to various locations.

After my release from jail, I moved in with my brother John, his three adult children, one minor child, and his wife Aretha who was employed by the state, where she worked with special-needs children. Retha, as she was called by the family, worked in Lyons and most of the time I caught a ride with her to work. Every now and then I'd ride back with her but generally I made other arrangements.

My brother John was also my drinking buddy, and every Friday, Saturday, and Sunday we drank and drank and drank. At the time, I felt as though I was having a ball, and you couldn't tell me that I wasn't living the life of Riley! John didn't ordinarily say a whole lot when he was sober, but when he drank, he had a tendency to tell you whatever was on his mind.

One day, John discovered that some money he'd had in his house was missing. No one had a clue what had happened. But Saturday night when we were drinking, John started to talk about the missing money. He wasn't accusing me of anything, but the fact of the conversation itself forced me to make a big decision about my life. I made the decision to move out on my own.

I got myself a room right there in Lyons, within walking distance to the shop. The Big Apple was a storefront with two rooms located on each side for $25 a week. The landlord, D. J. Singleton was always complaining that I was running his light bill up because of the small electric heater I used in my room. When I got my check, I gave him something extra for his electricity bill so that I wouldn't make him mad. DJ was that kind of person who would talk loudly and curse at you. But because he didn't like the heater, I had to endure a lot of cold nights. The only heat came from an antiquated wood stove in the middle of the house. Not only was DJ stingy with the heat, but he guarded the wood for the stove like a hawk. If you wanted to use the stove you had to cut your own wood.

One Friday night, my buddies and I decided to ride to Savannah to have a little fun. Somewhere along the way, we were stopped by the police for some reason. Perhaps it was because we were five black men in an automobile. Or it could have been the Toombs County plates on the car. The officer ran a check on each of us and they found there was an outstanding warrant for my arrest. I went to jail that night and stayed there the whole weekend until I could go to court on Monday morning.

I was very calm as I appeared again before Judge Karp. Court records determined that I had been arrested over a year ago and had already done my time for that DUI. Obviously, there was a glitch in the paperwork or the records had not been updated. I had to suffer like so many others whose paperwork got lost or mixed up in the shuffle of our legal system. As I look back on that time, I wonder, "If we had been five white men in a vehicle that night, would we have been stopped?" Probably not.

By now I had reached a low point in my life and I began to hang out behind the Main Street Grocery store with a bunch of fellows in Lyons. It was here that I would drink beer and whiskey on a daily basis. The package store was located right next to the grocery store and the easy access contributed to the popularity of the location. Through it all I continued to show up for work, as I had become a functioning alcoholic.

One rainy day as I was working in the shop with Mr. Martin, a fellow walked up to me and said, "You know, a lot of guys around here don't like a black man working here." He continued, "It doesn't bother me at all because I got a lot of black friends." At this time, I was the only black man working in the shop and I would imagine it was hard for some of those guys to make adjustments because of my presence. But Mr. Martin was different and he always came to my rescue when I needed him. Right at that moment, Mr. Martin called for me to join him on the road. As we drove away, I casually mentioned to him what I had just been told. He said, "Somebody probably pumped him up to say that to you."

I later learned that the federal government determined there were many counties that refused to adequately utilize blacks in the work-force, which was in violation of the Civil Rights Act of 1964 and equal employment opportunity. If the counties did not comply with the law, they would not have access to federal funds.

I realized that the county didn't hire me because they wanted to; they did it because the law required them to comply. I guess it was all about fulfilling the law and I was their token black employee.

On days when it rained, there was very little work in the shop, so most of the guys would just sit around idly. It didn't matter to them because they were on the clock and would be paid regardless. But Mr. Martin was the type of person who preferred to stay busy, so we would work on automobiles from the Sheriff's Department. Sometimes we brought the county's equipment into the shop and worked on it where it was dry. We were always working regardless of the weather.

Once, everyone but myself and Mr. Meek—an older gentleman who answered the telephone in the shop—had all been sent out on road jobs.

The road superintendent had an office right next to the shop and he walked in and said that he needed a heavy piece of equipment loaded onto the back of his truck. He hollered out my name. "Richard, I need you to put this steel bar on the back of my truck 'cause it's too heavy for my men!"

Too heavy for his men? I thought. All those big strong white men he had working for him? I was just a measly 145 pounds, at best. I did exactly as he commanded me but I was agitated about the way I had been treated. I was so angry that I walked off the job that day and went home to Savannah. I imagine Mr. Meeks told Mr. Martin what happened, because shortly thereafter Mel Taylor contacted me and assured me that nothing like that would happen again if I returned to work. He also told me that from now on, Mr. Martin would be the only person I had to answer to. With those assurances, I returned to work as usual on Monday morning.

Since I was the only black employee working at the shop affiliated with the jail, several of the brothers around Lyons decided I must be a snitch, especially since I wasn't from Toombs County. That was the rumor around town and a lot of people thought it was strange that the county would hire me. But most of them just didn't know the circumstances of my employment.

CHAPTER 8

AS I WAS WORKING with Mr. Martin on a well job one day, he looked at me and said in a sincere voice, "Richard, you are too good a fellow to let yourself go like this." I'm sure he said it because he smelled the alcohol I had drunk the night before and he had noticed my disheveled appearance. This hurt me because I truly respected Mr. Martin. In my heart, I truly wanted to get myself together. While I wasn't fully conscious of the effect that remark had on me, I found that I was becoming interested in Christian television. On Sunday mornings, I found myself watching Jimmy Swaggart and Frederick Price. I began to sense a change coming over me but the enemy wouldn't leave me alone.

One day I saw a woman walking with her three children and I decided to flirt with her. I asked her for her name and where she lived and she told me that she lived on the hill. I asked if I could stop by her house sometime and she told me I could. This would turn out to be the beginning of my relationship with Trace, who would become the mother of my third and final child, James.

I continued to visit Trace night after night until one night she invited me to spend the night; I did. This relationship continued in this way until I spent the weekend in Savannah and returned to find that Trace had moved all my belongings into her home. I was very angry because I was struggling daily to get myself together so that I could move back home to Savannah. Through it all, our relationship continued and Trace assured me that she was taking birth control pills. I trusted her, seeing no reason for her to lie to me.

Mr. Martin, who was both my supervisor and my friend, warned me that I needed to be careful. I told him, "We're just friends." Even so, within a year, I learned that Trace was pregnant with my son, James.

I was very angry when she approached me with the news because I felt like I had been betrayed. I had so many problems and issues in my life and I was not prepared to father another child.

To be totally honest, I was not ready to be a one-woman man because back home in Savannah, I was still seeing a woman I had been involved with for a few years. We saw each other every other weekend.

On one of those weekends in Savannah, my cousin James, his wife, and my lady friend decided to visit my sister in Miami. When I got back to Lyons, Trace wasn't at home. It didn't take long for me to find out that Trace had given birth. I was told she had gone to Augusta with the baby because he was born with complications to his bowels. When she returned home, I learned that my son, James, would have to undergo surgery. My infant son would need a colostomy bag for the first three years of his life.

Even after James was born, I continued with my Savannah affair, because I had no intention of getting married again. However, this bi-weekly relationship ended one night when I showed up at her back door on the wrong weekend. I knocked but she did not answer right away. I began to entertain all kinds of wild notions. When she finally opened the back door, I could see someone walking out the front door. We talked and she cried and tried to explain what had just happened, but after this incident, I decided to stay with Trace and take care of my son, James.

Even though I decided to be with Trace, I still had a desire to be with other women. Sitting in the Breakfast Shop one day, I spotted a woman named Marge. When I got the chance to say something to her, I couldn't resist. I causally suggested that she let me take her out to dinner one evening and she laughed. We both went our separate ways until I ran into her again at the Breakfast Shop. This time I gave her my phone number and she promised to give me a call. She did, and we decided one Friday night to drive to Swainsboro, Georgia.

We had dinner at the Western Sizzler and sat around talking about our lives. She was married, but according to her, they were separated. I knew who her husband was and I had heard that he was living with another woman. I didn't really consider her to be married until one evening I learned that someone had told her husband that we were involved.

Her husband went to see Trace in an attempt to find me. As fate would have it, I had gone to Savannah after I dropped Marge off that night. So when Trace called me to say the husband of some woman stopped by to tell her I was out with his wife, I was actually in Savannah.

When I returned home on Sunday, Trace confronted me about the woman. "Could I be in two places at once?" I asked her by way of defense. "How could I have been with another man's wife when you spoke to me while I was in Savannah?"

When I finally spoke with Marge, I learned that she had moved to Vidalia. We continued to see each other for about four years while I was still involved with Trace. During those years, I also got myself involved with another married woman named BJ.

I didn't know BJ personally but I had seen her around a few times. I never considered a relationship with her until she called me at work one day. "Hey, Ricky," she said, "I'd like to see you." I suggested we meet in Swainsboro and she agreed.

There was a period of time where I was involved with all three women at the same time. Things were going just fine until one night, a fellow who was interested in BJ spotted us on an isolated road. I can't say for sure, but I believe he got word to her husband because a short while later, BJ's husband showed up and caught the two of us in the backseat of her car.

We scrambled, got out of the car, and saw that BJ's husband held a butcher knife in one hand. BJ and her husband started to argue about who was cheating on whom. While they were distracted with their argument, I got into my truck and drove off. Later on, BJ continued to call me, and I suggested she get her affairs straight with her husband because he had started to show up at my work, making accusations. Yet through all of that, somehow she and I continued to see each other.

I had moved to Vidalia, Georgia, and every now and then I would see BJ's husband driving down my street. I assumed he was looking for his wife's car.

With all the problems I had to endure, it was easy for me to slip back into my old habits. I started drinking again and then I moved on to using drugs. I could no longer deny the fact that I needed help. So I decided to enroll in a drug rehabilitation program for seven days.

After I finished the program, I felt as though I was always fearful. I always felt that someone or something was watching me. I became extremely paranoid when Mel Taylor warned me to watch my company and extracurricular activities. Living in a small town, everyone knew everyone's business and I imagine he'd heard people talk about me. I was dipping and dabbing in illegal activities and I'm sure he had heard about it.

I went home to Savannah nearly every week and when it came time to make another trip, I went home, excited to catch up with my friends. I stopped by my tight man's house and discovered that someone else was living in his apartment. The current resident suggested that my buddy had left and gone to New York City. With that information I decided to visit my parents.

After spending some time with my parents, I went back to Toombs County and decided the seven-day program had been a waste of my time. I was still using drugs and felt as though I'd hit my lowest point. I spoke with Sheriff Charles Durst and confessed my addiction and told him I needed some help.

He told me about a 16-week program at a rehabilitation center called Anchorage in Albany, Georgia. This program was very strict and it was important that you were serious about it if you wanted it to work. My mother, Trace, and my Aunt Lavern all agreed to accompany me when I decided to enter the drug treatment program.

People came from all parts of Georgia trying to get clean. I remember how we had to listen to tapes by Pastor Charles Stanley of Atlanta.

This was my first introduction to this great teacher. To this day I continue to study and listen to Pastor Charles Stanley.

While I was in the program, the facilities' tractor broke down. Because they knew about my work history at the county, I was asked to fix the tractor.

About four weeks into the program I began to have problems with a tooth. It was a Friday and my tooth required an extraction, which meant that I would have to leave the center and return on Sunday. This was considered a strike against you because leaving the center would give you easy access to alcohol or drugs.

Some four weeks later I had to leave the treatment center again. I don't remember why, but I do know that I was not allowed to return. I had exhausted my two strikes and now I was out of the program.

I still had my job with Toombs County so I went back to work. At this time, the county had started hiring more black employees. Toombs County was trying to play catch-up because blacks had started to enter the political arena. A white female vacated her seat as commissioner and two blacks jumped on board. We elected our very first black county commissioner.

My entire life seemed like one great big mess. There was turmoil all around me. BJ decided to confront Trace one day about our relationship. I suppose she wanted to let Trace know we were seeing each other.

Shortly thereafter, Trace told me it was over between us and she started seeing someone else. As for me and Marge, we just sort of drifted apart. But BJ continued to call me and we continued our relationship, such as it was.

Around the shop things were pretty much the same. Racism was still alive and well and I was still treated the same as I had been. Mr. Martin, Mel Taylor, and James Lockley were the only guys who treated me as though I was somebody. James Lockley was a great inspiration to me. He knew of my situation and much of what I was going through and he was always offering words of wisdom and encouragement. He said to me one day after Trace and I had broken up, "Richard, you're letting your problems get you down." He suggested that whatever was bothering me might be helped if I went to the woman and told her I was sorry for whatever I had done. "If she accepts your apology, that's good," he told me. "If she doesn't, you move on because you've done your part."

I did exactly as he suggested and moved on with my life. Considering his words of wisdom, I realized that I had made several other mistakes in my past. I set out to make them right. I went to Elmira, the mother of my first child, and apologized for any pain I had caused her.

My life was full of trouble, and no matter which way I turned, trouble always seemed to be waiting for me around every corner. I was trying so hard to do the right thing and trying my best to stay out of trouble, but trouble just wouldn't leave me alone.

My nephew, Ward, stopped by my apartment one evening with a bottle of liquor. "Let's take a ride," Ward said. Realizing we would be drinking, I gave Ward the keys so that he could drive. I had a lot of experience driving under the influence and I was determined not to mess up and get my license taken away again.

As we drove around drinking, Ward spotted a woman he knew. Somehow, she ended up riding with us. The three of us rode around stopping by this club and that club. Somehow, the woman ended up with me in the back of my truck, which had a covered camper. Just as we were about to have consensual sex, blue lights began to flash all around us.

"Pull over, Ward," I said as I rushed to pull myself together.

As the police officer questioned us, the woman blurted out, "They raped me!" Ward and I looked at each other in shock at the lie. Why would she say such a thing? Somebody told us later that she was on probation and that she wasn't supposed to be out that time of morning. Even so, Ward and I were taken to the Vidalia jail where we spent three nights.

On Monday morning we were transferred to the Sheriff's Department in Lyons. One of the officers at the jail recognized me. "You know better than that," he said. We stayed in jail for five more days because the sheriff was out of town. Many of the prisoners knew that I worked for the county and someone said, "When Sheriff Durst comes back, he's gonna let you out." Sure enough, that's exactly what happened.

Sheriff Durst allowed me to sign my own bond and told me, "Go on back to work." Ward, on the other hand, wasn't able to get out of jail until someone paid his bond.

This incident lingered on for a while until the sheriff, who knew the woman and her history of making false accusations, told me. "You need to find someone who can talk to this woman and get her to tell the truth."

I learned that my sister-in-law knew someone who knew the woman's mother, and I convinced her to help me. She reached out to the woman's mother, who promised to talk to her daughter. She agreed to tell her daughter that if she told the truth about what happened, she would not be prosecuted for making false allegations. She agreed, and her mother drove the woman to the sheriff's office, where she dropped the charges.

On the following page is a copy of the dismissal of the charges:

IN THE SUPERIOR COURT OF TOOMBS COUNTY
STATE OF GEORGIA

STATE OF GEORGIA   *   W#9111671, Rape (Law)

                     *   Prosecutrix: Audrey Greene

v.   *

                     *   W#9111670, Rape (Mosley)

RICHARD LAW   *   Prosecutrix: Audrey Greene

and   *

WARD MOSLEY   *

DISMISSAL

The within warrants are hereby dismissed for the following reason: at the request of the complainant. Costs have been paid.

This 14ᵗʰ day of May, 1991.

_____
Richard A. Malone
District Attorney

Prepared by:

_____
Melvin E. Hyde, Jr.
Assistant District Attorney
Middle Judicial Circuit
P.O. Drawer J
Swainsboro, GA 30401
(912) 237-7846

State Bar No. 381425

Filed in office this ___15___
day of ___May___, 19_91_
                9 a M.
_____
Dep. Clerk Superior and State
Courts, Toombs County, Georgia

ATTEST: A TRUE COPY

Certified to __11/13__ 20_07_

_____
Deputy Clerk, Toombs County

50

CHAPTER 9

IT WAS COLD AND RAINY as we all stood around the gas heater located in the center of the shop. I stood near the heater with my arms behind my back as people chatted around me. I heard someone say, "Y'all know my niece. She's married to a black fellow and they got this here old black baby. I'd like to get a baseball bat and kill dat li'l old baby." Although I heard it very clearly, I felt no emotion whatsoever. I didn't even turn around. All I could do was stand still. In the back of my mind, I felt like the person who had spoken was hoping I would say something. But thanks to the God I serve and the God in me, I held my peace. Still, some things will never change.

A well-known proprietor stopped by the shop one day as the county was auctioning off some of its vehicles. As we all stood around outside, this man walked over to where Mr. Martin and I were standing. He reached around the front of me to shake Martin's hand, ignoring me completely. To me, this was disrespectful. I often endured disrespect from the people I worked with, so this was nothing new.

This man ran for chairman of commissioners and defeated Mel Taylor, the incumbent. Sometime after he was elected, the county hired a new employee. Rumor around the shop was that the new employee was the man's relative and had gotten his job through nepotism. This was a violation of the county's hiring procedure because hiring officials were not supposed to participate in the hiring of their relatives. But it didn't matter because they did what they wanted to do, regardless of the law.

By now I had been working for the county for about ten years. In 1993, I was being paid about $5.30 an hour. The new employee owned a muffler shop in town and even though he came in as a mechanic, he was not at all familiar with the work in the shop. In fact I caught him watching me many times to see what I was doing. Even so, he was being paid $10.00 an hour, which was probably as much as Mr. Martin was making at that time.

Unfortunately, Mr. Martin began to experience back problems and was laid up for a while due to back surgery. Although he was not at work physically, I spoke to him daily and he gave me instructions about handling various problems.

One day the chairman of commissioners came into the shop and requested that I put a muffler on a truck. This was not our normal procedure for muffler replacement. We sent our vehicles to a muffler shop for repair because it was less costly. Instead of complying with the chairman's request, I called Mr. Martin. He suggested I leave the matter alone because it would certainly be too expensive to work on a muffler in the shop. He said that he would handle this situation by contacting the chairman.

Of course, the new employee was familiar with working on mufflers because he owned a muffler shop. Maybe the chairman was trying to justify this person's employment, especially since he hadn't been hired through the proper channels. Whatever the reason, he did not take kindly to my disregard of his authority. Since I was not very popular with the white workers, I think they spoke about this incident among themselves. Since most of the guys didn't want me there in the first place, it was easy for them to make accusations. A few days after the incident, a handwritten note appeared on my paycheck. It read, "You said you did not work for James Thompson. I want you to see who signed your check." The note was signed James Thompson.

I contend with all my heart that I never said anything about not working for James Thompson. After gathering myself, I reached out to another black commissioner, Elder Roy Lee Williams, who was a friend of mine. He suggested we show the note to Mel Taylor, the former chairman. When he read the note, he said, "That's really dirty. How could someone put something like that on someone's paycheck?"

With that, Elder Roy Lee Williams suggested I make a copy of the note and the check. He said he would talk to an attorney the first chance he got. It wasn't long before he contacted the only black attorney in Vidalia at that time. I was able to retain him as my attorney. He asked that I not use his name, which I respected. I guess if I were him and I left me hanging like he did, I wouldn't want my name mentioned either.

Nevertheless, after this attorney agreed to represent me, he decided we would travel to Savannah and file a complaint with the EEOC. Roy Lee, who was also the pastor of Mosley Town Church of God and Christ, and his wife Sandra came along that day to support me in my efforts. I recall walking into the office of the EEOC accompanied by my attorney. I was greeted by a very nice woman who listened as I explained my troubles to her. She gave us all the required forms we needed to file a complaint, and she indicated that we would hear from them after they had completed the investigation. She went on to say that I did not need to worry about retaliation from my employer because it was against the law. *Against the law?* I thought to myself. *Really?* These people have been breaking the law for years and my problems certainly weren't going to stop them from retaliating.

I'd sure like to find that woman today so I could let her know how wrong she was. It's been years now and nobody except the Lord knows all I've had to endure after I filed that complaint. The entire process went further than she could have imagined because of the stroke and complications with my stomach. Add to that the fact that Toombs County refused to allow me any kind of disability compensation for nearly ten years, and it's been a very difficult road. I was a 40-year-old man who had worked for Toombs County for over 11 years when I became disabled, and I got nothing from the county until I was fifty. Now, I might be wrong, but I believe that's "against the law." I'm no attorney, but I do know that when a person suffers a disability while employed at a state job, they are entitled to disability compensation. I couldn't get help because I filed a complaint against the county and they didn't care if I lived or died. Yes, I struggled through it all, but God kept me and I'm still here.

After leaving the office of EEOC that day, we headed over to my parents' house, where my mother had prepared a wonderful meal just for us. The three of us, together with my attorney, sat around the table eating, talking, and laughing before returning to Vidalia.

By now Mr. Martin was back at work and his doctor had approved him for light duty. He was not able to do any heavy lifting because he was still recovering from his back surgery. I was so happy and pleased that my friend was back on the job because he was truly a good man and I enjoyed working with him being in his company.

The well service job was only on the weekends but sometimes the job required me to go down into a well. Since Mr. Martin was plenty older than me, he wasn't able to climb in and out of wells all day. But he was constantly reminding me of how he'd done it all the time when he was younger. He was always telling me, "Richard, I would never ask you to do something I wouldn't do myself," or "Richard, learn as much as you can." I truly respected him because of his wisdom and his knowledge. I extend the same admiration to Mel Taylor because he would also encourage me and tell me to learn all I could on the job.

One evening Mr. Martin and I were on our way to work on a well when he casually mentioned, "We had a visitor in the shop from the EEOC the other day." He went on to say, "I told those people everything that was going on around here." I started to feel good inside because I thought something good was about to happen in my life. It probably would have if my attorney had not kicked me to the curb. I regret that I didn't press on until I found someone who was interested in helping me.

CHAPTER 10

AS I STARTED TO WATCH more and more Christian television, I noticed that my spiritual life began to change. I found that I was drinking less and I started attending church on a regular basis. I was trying my best to stay focused and I began to trust God with all my troubles. I was determined to activate my faith. I found strength in God and adopted an attitude of praise. I began to connect with other folks at the church as well as several pastors in the community, while involving myself in various church services. The struggle was difficult because I would often feel my inner spirit tugging me back to where I used to be. Every day I fought to do the right thing. Through it all, I knew that my struggle was not against flesh and blood but against the powers of this dark world and the devil who had set out to keep me in shackles. Though I tried to stay involved in church, I often found myself slipping back into my old habits. I wanted so badly to do what was right.

On a Thursday night, I had my mind made up about what I wanted to do that weekend. I was planning to attend a three-night revival at the First African Baptist Church of Vidalia. Pastor Sam Davis was the revivalist for the evening and he preached straight from his soul.

At the end of the night, an older woman approached me and said, "You should have been up there on the pulpit." I don't know why she said that but I was determined to return the following night. I went back and enjoyed myself even more! My soul was on fire for the Lord and I felt truly revived. The last night of the revival, Mr. Martin had some work he needed to do and I felt obligated to help him so, unfortunately, I was unable to go.

As good as Mr. Martin had been to me and as much as I wanted to attend the final night of the revival, I could not say no to him when he asked me to help him pull a pump out of a well. The well was located on the outskirts of Lyons, all the way out in the country. We had to travel a few miles to get there.

As we began our journey, Mr. Martin decided to stop by the Coffee Shop to buy hamburgers for us to eat along the way. When we reached our destination, we began to change the pipes when all of a sudden Mother Nature called.

Moving slowly to the other side of the truck, I was able to relieve myself. "Richard, are you all right?" Mr. Martin asked as I returned, my coveralls wide open. It was the middle of January and I was burning up.

"I'm fine," I muttered. We finished the job and he dropped me off at BJ's house for the night.

BJ says that I fell asleep on the couch and she woke me up and told me to get ready for bed. Sometime around nine the next morning, I woke up and went into the bathroom. As I tried to speak, my words were slurred. I walked out of the bathroom and fell against the bathroom wall. BJ tried to help me back to bed. She asked me what was wrong but I couldn't reply. I smiled up at her but BJ could tell that something wasn't right. Again, I tried to speak but my words came out slurred.

BJ called her sister, who suggested she call an ambulance, which she did. When they arrived, she directed them to the bathroom, where they examined me and asked me various questions. BJ thought I might be having a stroke but when she asked the paramedic if that were possible, she was told that wasn't what was happening. Even so, BJ knew that something was very, very wrong.

BJ asked if the paramedics would take me to the hospital but, for some reason, they told her that it would be better if she drove me in her car. She didn't argue and took me to the emergency room. The doctors examined me but couldn't find anything wrong, so they left me in a room.

BJ called my mother and brother to tell them what was happening. My brother John and some of his friends came by the hospital to check on me.

BJ stayed with me at the hospital until they took me to Georgia Regional Hospital. It was a cold January morning and I didn't have any shoes, but no one seemed to care. The entire hospital staff showed very little concern for me that day. Perhaps they assumed I was using drugs because the questions they asked seemed to indicate that they suspected that. But I wasn't on any drugs.

The hospital contacted the police, who showed up and treated me as though I were a criminal. I didn't get the help I needed that day because Toombs County didn't try to help me at all.

BJ must have called my sister-in-law Aretha, who called my mother and told her I was being sent to the Georgia Regional Mental Health facility in Savannah. Retha said that someone needed to meet me there. "Georgia Regional?" my mother shouted. "What's he going there for? He's not crazy. Why in the world are they taking him there?" My mother, who was always calm, was worked up and agitated.

My mother, father, Aunt Thelma, and Uncle Cecil arrived at Georgia Regional Hospital. The woman at the desk asked, "Can I help you?"

No one replied. Instead, they walked straight ahead because my mother had caught a glimpse of me from the back. I was sitting in a chair facing a nurse who must have been trying to get information from me. Mama walked right up and stood in front of me. Immediately, my eyes lit up as I recognized her. But I said nothing. I still wasn't able to speak.

The woman at the desk smiled and said, "I'm so glad somebody came to see about him."

"He's not a throwaway," my mother said. "He's got people who care about him."

Since I was not able to speak, Uncle Cecil suggested they give me a pen and a piece of paper so that I could write things down. I took the pen and paper and attempted to write something. The nurse looked at the paper and said, "This is nothing but scribble."

Finally, the doctor arrived. As they were taking to me into the exam room, my mother decided to follow us. All of a sudden, the nurse yelled, "You can't go back there with the doctor!"

"It's okay," the doctor said. "Let Mom come on back."

My mother looked at the doctor and said, "I don't know what happened, but I do know he's not crazy." She continued, "Toombs County sent my child here in a police car. In all that cold with nothing on his feet but a pair of ankle socks. He didn't even have on a jacket." The doctor was kind and explained that the hospital in Vidalia was small and they probably hadn't done a thorough examination on me. Instead, they sent me to Georgia Regional Hospital.

My mother asked if the nurse had kept the piece of paper I'd had when they brought me in. The nurse said they did have it but that they needed to keep it. Mom asked to see it and as she looked, she was able to read the words, "This Sickness is a Blessing."

The attending physician at Georgia Regional Hospital determined that my family needed to transport me to the emergency room at Memorial Medical Center. Upon arrival, I was immediately admitted as a patient.

Because my mother was not able to tell the doctors what had happened to me, she assured them that as soon as she got back home, she was going to call Vidalia and learn the details of my illness. At this point, my family had been at the hospital for some time so my father and Cecil went home while Aunt Thelma stayed with Mom. I'm told that my condition was pretty bad because I was sent to the ICU.

The nurse on duty told my mother to let them know if she was going to leave because they did not expect me to make it through the night. They said my chances of survival were 50-50. The devil was out to kill me, but all glory to God who turned it around for my good. The hospital staff said one thing but God said, "Not so, not on my watch."

The next morning, I was still unable to speak but I was alive. God was on my side and it wasn't going to be over until God said so. He was not through with me yet because God had a plan for my life. There was still work for me to do.

Mama stayed with me until I was out of danger. Then she went home to make those phone calls. Sitting down to call my sister-in-law Aretha, she was determined to understand why the family had allowed me to go through this alone. "Why didn't somebody come with him?" Mama asked. Retha didn't really have an excuse but she did tell Mama that my brother John was too drunk to have come.

Next on Mama's call list was BJ, who said I stayed in the bathroom so long that she became concerned and decided to check on me. She told Mama, "When I opened the door he was turning around in circles as though he was lost, so I helped him get in the bed and he was able to lay down." BJ told Mama that the next morning when I didn't wake up, she thought I was having a stroke because one of my arms appeared limp. BJ told Mama she called 911 and the ambulance arrived shortly. She told the paramedics right away that my arm was limp. "I asked if they thought he was having a stroke," BJ told Mama. "They said, 'No, he's not.'"

BJ told Mama that she asked if I was going to be taken to the hospital and she was told, "You can take him yourself." She told my mom, "We managed to get to Meadows Memorial Hospital, where the medical staff was insensitive to Ricky's condition." She explained that they took their sweet time in seeing me.

BJ explained that when someone finally came to my room, they decided it was necessary to contact the Sheriff's Department, which is how I ended up at Georgia Regional Hospital.

I guess everything happens for a reason because if they hadn't sent me to Savannah, I might have died in Toombs County because I was so sick. We learned later that according to the doctors, I was having a stroke after all. BJ had been right.

Today I am grateful that the physician at Georgia Regional examined me thoroughly and transferred me to Memorial Hospital. I was hospitalized for seven days, and upon my release, I was required to come back regularly for a blood test and speech therapy.

Mama was right there for me through everything, looking after me and taking care of me. She took me to all my appointments and never once complained.

During my illness, no one from my job tried to contact me except Mr. Martin. I'm told he came to visit while I was intensive care. Sometime later, he told me that he thought I was going to die. I'm so glad that God kept me so that one day I could tell my story.

CHAPTER 11

AFTER BEING RELEASED from the hospital, I remained under a doctor's care. Right after my discharge the hospital began to ask how I planned to pay for the care and treatment I'd received. I knew that insurance payments were taken out of my weekly check. I tried to explain that to Martha Kraft, who worked in the accounting department at Memorial. I couldn't make myself clear to her, so Mama took charge and spoke for me. Ms. Kraft was kind enough to call Toombs County on my behalf to obtain the name of the insurance company. However, the person she spoke with refused to give her any information.

By now, nearly everyone at my job was talking about my illness and the complaint I had filed with the EEOC. Family members were suggesting that my illness was brought on due to the harassment from my job. Maybe this is the reason I couldn't get any answers to my questions about my insurance with Blue Cross Blue Shield. Maybe this was their retaliation against me.

When Roy Lee, my friend and a commissioner, advised me that the county was considering cancelling my insurance, I made it my business to pay my monthly premiums out of pocket. I knew if I was not actively working, the county wouldn't be responsible for paying my health insurance. For that reason I gave Mr. Martin and sometimes Roy Lee money to pay my insurance premiums. On April 1, 1994, the following letter was sent to the county on my behalf:

Memorial Medical Center, Inc.

April 1, 1994

Mr. Richard H. Law
DOB ~~10-11-51~~
SS No. ~~xxx-xx-xxxx~~
MMC No. 01737007

Mr. Richard Law has been followed at Memorial Medical Center as an In and
Out Patient since 1-8-94. Diagnosis is Cardiovascular Accident with
generalized weakness and speech aphasia. Mr. Law is receiving Speech and
Occupational therapy as an Out patient. He is also on Coumadin Medication
Therapy which will be necessary for approximately 6 more months. While on
Coumadin Therapy Mr. Law will not be able to return to his prior employment.

Your assistance in helping Mr. Law continue on with his health insurance
coverage until he is able to resume work would be greatly appreciated.

Please advise if further information is required.

Respectfully,

Dr. T. Gongaware
Medical Director
Out Patient Clinic

MMC Contact: Mary Lou Henderson LMSW
Social Worker
(912) 350-8589

P.O. Box 23089
Savannah, GA 31403-3089

It wasn't long after this letter was received that Mary Lou Henderson, a social worker at the hospital, applied for Social Security for me. The doctors had already determined I was going to be out of work for six months or more. I had no money or any funds coming in.

I was denied Social Security and I felt as though I had no choice but to try and go back to work. But within two weeks I found myself back in the hospital. I began to have excruciating pains in my stomach but I didn't want to go back to Meadows Memorial.

I was going to Savannah to get help but BJ suggested I let them check me out before I traveled all the way to Savannah. While I was waiting to be seen, Dr. Clark walked in. I guess he'd heard about the difficulties I'd encountered the last time I was there because he apologized. After explaining my stomach issues, he assured me he would take care of me. Dr. Clark took very good care of me; he is an excellent physician.

After taking X-rays, he determined that I needed emergency surgery for an abscess I had developed. He performed the surgery and I was hospitalized for seven days.

On the second day of my hospital stay, Dr. Clark told me, "I called that doctor down in Savannah and told him he should have never given you those coated aspirins. Those aspirins caused a hole in the lining of your stomach."

Because of my numerous complications, Dr. Clark suggested a follow-up with my doctor in Savannah after I was discharged. I followed up with Dr. Kollias, who worked in the clinic. He examined me and gave me a prescription for Zantac. He also told me that he was moving to practice in Texas. I wasn't in Savannah long before I remembered another doctor's appointment I had made in Vidalia with Dr. Patterson in an office building owned by Dr. Smith.

When I arrived, I was told that Dr. Patterson was no longer in Vidalia. Instead, I was seen by Dr. Barber, who was extremely rude and obnoxious. I don't remember the exact details of this appointment, but I know that someone said they were going to check my heart. When I realized they were going to put me to sleep, I began to get very nervous.

Dr. Barber leaned down and said, "We're gonna watch you," which made me even more nervous. It's not easy living in a small town like Vidalia where everyone knows your business. I'm sure everyone knew about my complaint against James Thompson.

My commissioner friend Roy Lee and his wife Sandra were very compassionate during my various illnesses. They were kind enough to open their home to me and allowed me to live with them as I recuperated. The love and kindness they extended to me went above and beyond the call of duty. They treated me like a member of their family and I shall be forever grateful to them.

Shortly thereafter, I received papers in the mail and a phone call from the office of EEOC. I was told that everything was in order and I could proceed with my complaint. At that moment, I felt as though a heavy load had been lifted from my shoulders. Still trying to recuperate, I became very cautious in my conversations with the people I came into contact with, particularly concerning this matter. I watched my every word.

If all my health and financial complications weren't enough to deal with, I received additional news that depressed me. I stood on Roy Lee's porch and saw my attorney drive by. I waved, and he stopped to chat. As I began to pour my heart out to him, I told him I had been hospitalized twice. I had a stroke and then because of stomach problems I went back to the hospital a second time. Right then, without any emotion, he told me that he could no longer represent me. He said, "I'm starting a new job in Savannah as the assistant district attorney and I can no longer represent you because that would be a conflict of interest." This took a whole lot out of me. I was at a loss for words and didn't really know what to do. When I think back to that day, I realize he never once suggested another attorney or referred me to anyone else.

I understand that this man had a job with a regular salary he could depend on. He no longer needed me and my case. But why would he treat me this way, especially when he knew I was depending on him? Perhaps that's the reason he does not want his name mentioned.

I did try to talk to a couple of other attorneys but I was unsuccessful because I didn't have much money. Nevertheless, several years later as I began to gather notes and details of my complaint, I learned that the EEOC only kept files for a certain number of years. My wife suggested that I contact the same attorney, who might still have records or some information concerning the outcome of the lawsuit I had filed against Toombs County. He responded by saying he could not remember anything because it had been too long. He said, "When I was retained by Richard Law, I was in private practice and that's been over 14 years ago." To me, it seems odd that he could remember how long ago he had been my lawyer but nothing about the details of the case. He ended the conversation with my wife by saying that he could not talk with her about this case so she passed the phone to me. We spoke briefly but he never once asked why I was contacting him. The bottom line is that the lawyer did not want to talk with me. But it's all okay because God is still able and he brought back to my memory the day my attorney drove me to Savannah to file my complaint.

CHAPTER 12

AFTER THE SETBACK with my stomach issues, I found myself unemployed again. I was determined to go home. When I got back to Savannah, Mama told me I had a letter from Social Security waiting for me. The letter included forms that I needed to fill out and return. Since I was going to the hospital anyway, I took the papers with me and asked Ms. Kaye Denham, a very kind and caring social worker, to help me complete them.

Finally, after my second appeal, I was approved for Social Security. What a wonderful blessing from the Lord! I know it was the Lord because the Social Security Administration went back and calculated the figures from the period when I was employed at Union Camp. My Social Security check would be more than the amount of money I was making while employed for Toombs County. This reminds me of the song by Doris Akers, "You just can't beat God's giving, no matter how you try."

After months of speech therapy I was able to pronounce words again, and slowly, I began to heal. I stayed in my room for about two months and didn't come out except to eat. During that time I watched so many videotapes and television ministries of Bishop T. D. Jakes, Creflo Dollar, Bishop I. V. Hilliard, Charles Stanley, and a local preacher named Ken Hall from Coastal Cathedral. I continued to read God's word, and through faith, the Lord began to heal my body.

Below is a letter Kaye Denham wrote on my behalf.

April 17, 2009

I first met Richard after he had his stroke and was coming to the day rehabilitation program to receive intensive out patient therapy services to begin his recovery. I remember meeting with him and his mother when he was admitted. He had experienced a terrible stroke, which impacted his communication and speech skills. He had lost his job and had applied for social security disability benefits. He was living with his mother and she took care of his needs and brought him to receive therapy.

Richard was experiencing the loss of all those things we all count on. A job, financial security, and people dropping out of his life as a result of having such a life threatening illness..

To add insult to injury, he was denied for social security disability benefits .We had to appeal this decision several times. Richard bore this all with grace, but was obviously very discouraged and met with huge disappointments from the system as a whole.

I remember him very quietly working to heal from his stroke. He suffered from the sadness and depression that accompany having to live with a blow like this. He had to learn to communicate again from scratch and this was often disheartening and difficult.

He continued to persist and over time was able to gain the skills he needed to speak with confidence and rebuild his life.

He continued to work each day to develop the abilities the stroke had so brutally taken from him. He completed the day rehabilitation program and continued to work toward recovery as he continues to do to this day.

He has found strength and courage to reach out and help others. He has learned new skills, he has married a lovely woman, Johnnie Mae, and he now volunteers in his community to encourage others. I am privileged to have been a part of his life when he was at his lowest and I find inspiration in watching him live daily in the service of God in the present.

I look forward to seeing where his ministry will take him in the future.

Kay Denham

Kay Denham, LMSW,OSW-C

Mama hosted a Home Bible Study every Monday at the house and I became a part of this ministry. The teachers, Evangelist Ernestine Brown and Minister Johnnie Mae Richards, prayed for me and with me often. Every day I felt like I experienced a calling for my life. God had cleansed me for a purpose and I know it was because he was preparing me to minister and witness to others. My cousin Pastor Jamie Shuman would often encourage me with words of inspiration as we sat around talking about the Lord.

Deep within my spirit, I wanted to regain the knowledge and all I lost after the stroke. My ability to pronounce words was gone. I could tie my shoes but I couldn't say, "I need to tie my shoes." I could use my fork to eat, but I couldn't say, "Pass me a fork, please."

My daughter Chassidy witnessed my struggles and suggested I enroll in Richard Arnold's Adult Education School. I took her advice and in July of 1997 I received a certificate of Excellent Academics from Richard Arnold. This was still not enough, because I needed additional help with language and words. Through it all, I continued to study the Bible daily, which became a major contributing factor to my ability to enunciate words.

Attending church services on Sunday mornings became part of my routine, as I only had to walk around the corner to Mt. Zion AME, where Elliot Sams was the pastor. Right next to Mt. Zion AME was my grandmother's home. Next door to her was my family's church, Mt. Bethel Missionary Baptist Church where I sometimes worshipped. Then one day, my cousin James Williams invited me to fellowship with him at St. Paul CME Church, where the pastor was Henry R. Delaney, Jr.

The service was great and I felt right at home because I'm always at home in the house of the Lord. As the choir sang powerfully, I saw a very familiar face singing her heart out. It was my old friend Johnnie Mae. As fate would have it, immediately after the service she came over to welcome me and we talked briefly.

We both seemed pleased to see each other and as we prepared to leave, Johnnie Mae said, "Why don't you call some time?" I turned it around and suggested that she should call me. She took my number and said that she would.

Months passed and I attended the church service again and again. One evening, I was surprised when the phone rang. Johnnie Mae had finally called! We talked and talked and I learned that she was going through a divorce. I told her about my illnesses and we exchanged stories about our lives. It was obvious that we were both striving to live godly lives. She told me that she could tell I had changed when she witnessed me praising God in church. "It was as though a light was shining all around you, and I knew you were a changed person," she said.

During one of our conversations, I invited Johnnie Mae to the Monday evening Bible study at Mama's house. She promised to come and one evening she did! It was obvious she enjoyed the Bible study because she wasn't shy with words and she came back again and again.

We began to hold our very own private Bible study over the phone in the evenings. After we'd finish discussing the Bible, our conversations turned to personal things, and I told her all about the trials and tribulations I had been through in my suit against Toombs County. After I told Johnnie Mae about the way I was treated, she offered to read some of the paperwork I had. I got the packet to her, and once she read it, she knew instantly that I had a case. "This clearly states that payment of a disability pension is permitted," she told me and pointed out the relevant section.

"Right after the Social Security Administration issued you a letter stating you would receive disability benefits," Johnnie Mae explained, "Toombs County should have started sending you a check." I asked her if she would mind contacting Toombs County on my behalf. She began corresponding with them via the telephone and certified mail immediately. They told her that I had to be at least 50 years old in order to receive benefits. However, they were ignoring the adoption agreement, which had been in effect while I was employed.

We communicated for several years until finally I contacted the trustee who was responsible for the disbursement of funds. The articles under Disability Pension were so confusing that they were forced to contact a law firm for an explanation. The law firm concluded that Toombs County was in the right.

Needless to say, I wasn't satisfied with the conclusion, because I had been employed by Toombs County for over ten years. I was working for them during the time of my stroke, which was likely brought on because of the retaliation I received after I filed the EEOC complaint.

By now there were at least two different copies of the Toombs County defined benefit pension plan being circulated. With all the confusion regarding the interpretation, Toombs County was forced to rewrite a clearer plan, which now states: "If you qualify for disability, your first check is payable the latter of: Age 50, or effective date of the first Social Security Disability monthly benefit." Before this new plan, article 7.03 stated: "permits payment of the Participant's disability pension at any time after the Participant terminates employment because of disability," which is much more complicated!

It's all very clear and I shall never forget the way I was treated by Toombs County. Their racist treatment and attitude toward me is the reason I have decided to tell my story. I hope and pray if you are reading this book and you or someone you know has experienced a similar situation, they can benefit from my story and will not have to endure the struggles that have caused me so much pain.

In an effort to compile the files and records Toombs County had on me, I learned that most of them are now missing. I believe in my heart that if I had been a white man, I would have immediately received disability payments. But for some reason, Toombs County has always had two sets of rules: one set for whites and another for blacks. I didn't know what my rights were, so I was tossed aside and wasn't given any help. I pray and believe that they will one day make restitution and I will receive all the money that's due me, plus interest. But then again, we all know that some things will never change.

CHAPTER 13

AS GOD CONTINUED TO ALLOW ME to wake up each morning, I couldn't get the thought of getting out of Savannah out of my mind. I was in desperate need of a vacation so I decided to visit my sister and brother-in-law, Dot and Marvin Deshazior, in Miami. After being in Miami for two weeks I decided to visit my niece Shelia Deshazior in Key West. I stayed down there for a few days before she decided she was going home to Miami. Shelia was a member of Antioch Missionary Baptist Church where Pastor Arthur Jackson III is a dynamic preacher and teacher. I enjoyed the services so much that whenever I'm in Miami I make it my business to worship there. I enjoyed Pastor Jackson so much that I have on several occasions purchased CDs and DVDs from the church.

I stayed away for nearly two months and spent most of my time thinking about Johnnie Mae and the friendship we'd rekindled. I thought about her a lot . I think that Johnnie Mae did a lot of thinking also because right after her divorce, our friendship seemed to grow. In February of 1998 we went out to dinner for the very first time. Perhaps we saw this as a celebration for us, but we did not go alone. We invited my mom and my aunt Ruth and they accompanied us to a lunch buffet at the Desoto Hilton.

As time passed, Johnnie Mae and I grew closer and spent more and more time together. The most interesting thing about our relationship was that we were both devoted to God and the fear of God would not allow us to so much as kiss or touch each other inappropriately. We had known each other in the past but I wanted the past to stay in the past; I think we both did.

I often asked Johnnie Mae, "How do you feel about me?" Of course, she would turn the question right back around on me. We went back and forth like this until one day, we both overcame our fear and doubt and confessed our love to each other.

I remember trying to express my love in June of 1998. Johnnie Mae was taking her mom, who lived in Hardeeville, South Carolina, to Ridgeland, South Carolina, to handle some business, and she asked me to ride with her. I was always happy to be in her company so I said yes right away. I told myself that a lot of things could happen in Ridgeland so I better be prepared for something extraordinary to happen.

Richard & Johnnie Mae Law

When Johnnie Mae picked me up, I came to the door in a suit jacket and she wondered why I was so dressed up. I approached her side of the car and said, "Since we're going to Ridgeland, we might as well get married!" I could tell that she was totally at a loss for words. She had just gone through a divorce and I knew that she didn't want to get married again. I knew that she had just gotten out of an abusive relationship six months prior. I knew that she enjoyed being in my company and I suspected that she might even be in love with me, but I knew that marriage was nowhere on her agenda in the near future.

Even knowing all that, I think I expected her to say, "Sure, let's get married." She must have been able to tell from my face that her response surprised me. She tried to explain that her first marriage to her children's father had failed because they were just babies when they had babies of their own. She also said that her second marriage was a big mistake because she married someone who deceived and abused her. She said that it was nothing more than a contractual relationship that she didn't want to remember for the rest of her life.

Whenever she would discuss her marital problems with me, I would always tell her to pray about it. I thought that might have been frustrating for her—perhaps she wanted to hear something more than "Just pray, Johnnie Mae." But she told me she continued to pray and we remained close friends.

It wasn't long before we both realized that we loved the Lord equally and we were destined to be together. So, despite Johnnie Mae's initial reservations, on September 3, 1998, Elder Charlie Williams married us. We needed a witness so Johnnie Mae called her friend and coworker Deloris Phoenix. She hesitated at first but eventually she came to our aide. Thinking back on it, we didn't tell anyone that we were planning on getting married. We went to the Health Department and got blood tests and applied for our marriage license at the courthouse.

After we were married, we decided it was time to tell everyone. We went to tell my parents first, and my mother said only, "Oh." I don't remember if she said anything at all. Despite the lukewarm reactions of our families, I know that, aside from the Lord, we are the best thing to ever happen to each other.

Richard and Johnnie Mae with four of their children and one grandchild

As the years passed, our parents grew to love both of us and they soon realized we were meant for each other. My father loved Johnnie Mae and we soon realized that she could get him to do many things that other folks couldn't. My mom loves her as if she'd given birth to her. They're so close that we joke about Johnnie Mae being my mother's daughter and I'm the son-in-law. My sister is also thrilled to have her very own sister for the first time.

I know my mother-in-law, Vivian Walker, who went home to be with the Lord on Christmas Eve of 2012, loved me as well. Before she became ill, I would often ride over to Hardeeville without Johnnie Mae to check up on her. Many times I'd have to look for her because she wouldn't be at home. I never had to look very far because she never drove any further than the Post Office or the grocery store. Occasionally, she would drive to Ridgeland to the Piggly Wiggly grocery store. I will always remember her banana pudding that she made from scratch and how she would make one for me for no reason at all.

During my sickness, the Lord called me to work for him. He placed the need in my spirit to help get the word out about Him. I shared this vision with Johnnie Mae and she created cards for me to share with others. For many years, I had known in my heart that I was just an unknown individual, trying to tell the people I met about a man named Jesus who could save us all. The message on the card read:

These cards were a blessing to most people, but some of them did not appreciate them. I just pray for those people.

As Johnnie Mae and I grew closer to the Lord, we accepted our calling as ministers. We gave our initial sermons together in the fall of 2003 under the late Rev. Dr. Henry R. Delaney at St. Paul CME Church.

My ministry led me to visit many churches and allowed me to meet one of the greatest pastors I have ever known, Reverend Bennie Mitchell. I would describe Reverend Mitchell as a General for the Lord. He was not only the pastor of Connors Temple Baptist Church but a renowned community and civil rights activist who was both a gifted preacher and talented vocalist. I was always inspired by the way he preached to the political arena. He made it clear to elected officials that they had been elected by and for the people. Bennie Mitchell was instrumental in changing the political scene in Savannah. In December of 1995, we elected our first black mayor, Floyd Adams, Jr. (deceased).

This was a big adjustment for both blacks and whites. Savannah was predominantly black with many racial barriers but it was long overdue for a black mayor. When most cities began to name a street after Dr. Martin Luther King, Savannah was slow about jumping on board. Bennie Mitchell led the way, and West Board Street became Martin Luther King Jr. Blvd. Reverend Mitchell led the way with the first MLK parade in Savannah but never received the credit. I am so glad to say he was my friend. Whenever I visited his church, he never failed to acknowledge me.

Pastor and activist Bennie Mitchell

Connor's Temple Baptist Church, Inc.

Charlie Hall
Chairman of Deacons

509 Gwinnett Street at M.L. King, Jr., Boulevard • Savannah, Georgia 31401
Phone (912) 232-8291 • Fax (912) 232-8050

Louis Fair, Jr.
Chairman of Finance

Rev. Dr. Bennie R. Mitchell, Jr., Pastor

Beatrice Y. Mack
Church Clerk/Administrative Assistant

"A Church of Love, A Church of Truth"

January 6, 2009

As you read this autobiography of Mr. Richard Law, you will have to appreciate the many sacrifices he made. He is indeed an unknown soldier, and he helped to obtain many of the civil rights we enjoy.

We applaud Bro. Law for taking the time to chronologically record the sacrifices, hurt and pain he suffered personally and his family the same. We hope that you will, in reading the autobiography have been blessed, as I have been, as I read it and that it will inspire you to do what you can and where you can in your own setting.

Sincerely,

Rev. Dr. Bennie R. Mitchell, Jr.
Pastor

CHAPTER 14

SHORTLY AFTER MY INITIAL SERMON, the Ogeecheeton-Dawes Neighbor Association elected me as their president and I organized the very first community reunion, something that had always been in my heart. I had grown up in this community, as had so many others I had known over the years who had since moved away. Ogeecheeton had once been home to many people and it was my vision to see everyone reconnect and come together once again with lots of food, fun, and fellowship. This first community reunion was such a success, we decided to make it an annual event held every year on the Saturday before Mother's Day.

Ogeecheeton - Dawes
Annual Mother's Day Reunion

Because I was president of the neighbor association, I wanted to learn as much as I could. I attended many seminars offered by the city and used them as a learning tool to become familiar with the way neighbor associations operated. I was determined to familiarize myself with the various programs and assistance that were available for the community.

I continue with this work to this day and find it very fulfilling. Currently, I am working with the city on a new welcome sign that will be placed at the entrance to the community. We are also working on getting a historical marker for the community. As one of the historic Westside African-American communities in Savannah, the Ogeecheeton community developed and expanded primarily during the first half of 20th century and was reshaped by the city rezoning project in 1960s. The history of Ogeecheeton paved the way for the residents to fight for their civil rights while pursuing a better life. After the civil war, Chatham County expanded in size and organized more farm lots to the south, which were tied to the same ward pattern originally laid out by Oglethorpe during the establishment of Savannah. The land of the Ogeecheeton community today is part of farm lots, and in 1910, Ogeecheeton was laid out for Willis W. Wilder by E. J. Thomas, the civil engineer and county surveyor at the time.

With the aid and assistance of Alderman and Mayor Pro Tempore Van Johnson we are in the process of getting the playground extended and adding a screened pavilion with tables and chairs.

My community involvement afforded me the opportunity to attend an affair for Cathy Cox at Johnny Harris's Restaurant. Cathy was vying to become governor of Georgia and Deanie Frazier, a longtime friend and classmate of my wife, encouraged me to attend. It was there that I was introduced to Cathy Cox and State Representative Lester Jackson. Lester and I became friends and I worked on two of his campaigns. He is now Senator Lester Jackson for the State of Georgia. I was invited to his swearing-in ceremony, where I met a number of people who worked in the legislature. At the invitation of Dr. Jackson, I attended the Georgia Legislature's Black Caucus event in Atlanta.

Sen. Jack Hill and Richard Law, Sr.

Sen. Jackson, Governor Purdue, and Richard

As president of the neighborhood association, it was often difficult for me to conduct the community meetings as I wanted to. At first, I called on my close friend Gus Johnson or my wife to assist me. There was no denying that the stroke had affected my speech but I longed to improve my speech and control my fear. So in 2006 I enrolled in a class on public speaking and fearless presentations at the Armstrong Center. After I completed the class, I decided I needed additional training and I enrolled in several classes at Savannah Technical College. I took English and math just to challenge myself until I decided that none of that was going to change my life in a positive way. What I had lost was gone forever but I believed the Holy Spirit would teach me all the things I needed to know as well as restore my memories that had been lost.

And that's exactly what happened. I was led by the Lord to get involved in several community activities. As a Head-Start Policy Council representative, I attended meetings and events like emergency preparedness hosted by Congressman John Barrow. This was a very informative learning experience that taught community leaders how to be ready to respond in case of a weather-related disaster.

As my work in the community grew, I had an even greater desire to become more involved. I volunteered as a board member for the City of Savannah Historic District Review Board, where I served for three years.

Richard and Mayor Otis Johnson

Soon after, I received an invitation to become part of the Hungry Club Forum of Savannah. I learned about their interest in community education, issues, and cultural enrichment programs, so I was happy to get involved. Through this affiliation, I became the vice president of the organization and I met a lot of interesting and involved people.

One in particular was the Honorable Joseph Lowery, who had been a guest speaker during a banquet hosted by the Hungry Club. I had the pleasure of driving him back to his hotel, during which we talked a great deal about issues that were important to both of us and the community. It was an honor to speak with one of the greatest civil rights leaders around.

Left to right: Richard Law, Sr., Joseph Lowery, and Johnnie M. Law

Several years later, I would meet him again while visiting my daughter, Angel, and son in law, Kevin, of Atlanta. They are members of Cascade United Methodist Church, as is Joseph Lowery! I was pleased to see him again because God has truly blessed him with longevity.

On another occasion, I had the opportunity to meet Governor Roy Purdue and Lieutenant Governor Casey Cagle, which was an honor. Through it all, my aim and focus was always to best equip myself to improve my speech and become more knowledgeable about community affairs.

Joseph Lowery and Richard Law at Cascade United Methodist Church

Governor Roy Purdue and Richard Law, Sr.

Dorothy Pelote, Richard Law, Sr. and Congressman John Conyers

Senator Lester Jackson, Richard Law, Sr., and Casey Cagle

(Left to right) At the Savannah Civic Center standing is Richard Law, Jr., Tonea Stewart from"The Heat of The Night", Richard Law, Sr. and grandson, Jalen Gordon. Seated is a customer getting his hair cut.

My journey in life has given me the opportunity to acquaint myself with many people, but one stands out more than any other. Maybe I was drawn to him because we share the same last name. He was a brilliant man of integrity with a humble spirit. He was a man who didn't mind stooping down to pick up pieces of paper on the ground in the Ogeecheeton community. He cared enough to send a birthday card and cash to my 100-year-old grandmother. He was a man whose legacy is etched in the minds of many in Savannah and beyond. My wife describes him as a man who didn't mind opening the door for a woman who was giving him a ride. She said he was a gentlemen from the old school who still tipped his hat when greeting a woman.

Mr. W. W. Law was a phenomenal man who served as president of the NAACP in Savannah for more than 26 years. Mr. Law never drove an automobile, even when he worked as a letter carrier. Johnnie Mae said he took the bus to or from his route until the Postal Service began to transport letter carriers to their destinations. Often I would see him waiting at the bus stop after he retired and I happily stopped to give him a ride. It was a joy and an honor being in his company as he mesmerized me with his stories. He knew everyone on his mail route by name, children and adults alike. Mr. Law would tell me who grew up in a particular house and who the new owners were. His stories about the life and history of Savannah left me in awe. By the time I reached his destination, I would have undergone an educational lesson I would never forget. I am truly proud to have known such a great man.

W. W. Law.
Photo courtesy of Remer K. Pendergraph.

Over the years, many people have asked me if I am related to this great man. I can only report what a historian told me: "There are three groups of families in Savannah with the last name Law, and you are all related."

CHAPTER 15

AS TIME HAS PASSED, I've become a bit more comfortable speaking out about what I want to say. Perhaps it still takes me a little longer to get my point across, but when everything is said and done, most people know what I've said and they know that I've meant it. I am a man of my word.

As I began to get more involved in many community activities, I realized that it didn't take a master's degree to realize that the Ogeecheeton-Dawes community had been overlooked by the city and the county for years.

Upon entering the neighborhood, you are immediately greeted by a junkyard to your right. Junk cars can be seen everywhere you look. At Ogeecheeton's back door sits a concrete block company that constantly blows cement, sand, gravel, and all sorts of hazardous fumes and chemicals. The city has made us promises on top of promises but these obstructions still exist in our community.

Years ago, the auto parts store was called Ogeechee Wrecking Company but was better known as "the Junk Yard." Most of the company's property was located on Dawes Avenue. However, over the years, the entire junkyard was moved into our community piece by piece.

According to my mother, who turned ninety this past March, at one time there were houses in the same place where the junkyard sits today. "Lucille Brown, Ike and Doe Carter were residents back then,"

Mom told me. "My aunt Lizzie lived back there and you know what? There was a lane at one time in between those houses." It seems to me if a lane was located where the junkyard is; some of that property belongs to the city. But the City of Savannah has heard our complaints and I am hopeful that this issue will be resolved one day soon.

The problem I'm having is that I'm pretty sure that if Ogeecheeton was a white community, Savannah would never in a million years allow a junkyard to move into the community. But it's like I've said from the start, "Some things will never change." Racism is still alive in the 21st century.

As a leader in this community, I've been very vocal about this matter because Ogeecheeton had been an established community long before either of these businesses were allowed to move in. As a matter of fact, Ogeecheeton was laid out in 1910. The area consisted of a few homes, a dairy farm, fields, and wetland. Wilder's wife produced the design for the Savannah city flag, which is still in use today.

The Ogeecheeton community was known as "the Bottom," while Dawes Avenue was called "the Hill." Jesse Kearse, a prominent black plumber, placed the first deep-well water pump in his mother's back-yard. At that time the only water in the community came from handheld pumps. Not long after, Jesse decided he would extend his well-water pump throughout the neighborhood.

Eloise Law, my grandmother, was Jesse's first customer. In 1972, he charged her nine dollars to extend a water line from his water distribution system out of his mother's yard. It was not until August of 1974 that the county commissioners approved a water system for Ogeecheeton, and this only happened after Jesse Kearse requested that the county either give him an exclusive franchise for water service or pay him for providing water to the community.

Mr. Brown had a store on the corner of Dawes Avenue where everyone hung out. If we weren't there, we could be found at the Seashell House, formerly Southside Restaurant. Next door to the Seashell House was Tucker's Trailer Park, where only white residents lived. It's still standing today, but the residents are now mostly Hispanic.

Additionally, the Atlantic Railroad Company played a major role in the economy and growth of the area by employing many of the Ogeecheeton residents.

There were also major flooding issues on Dawes Avenue due to a drainage problem at Industrial Park. Several industrial companies came in and were allowed to set up shop right next door to the Dawes Avenue residents. Unfortunately, the Industrial Park was built at a higher elevation than Dawes Avenue, which caused rain to flow downhill into the homes of most of the residents. Many homes were ruined. This problem was so damaging that I reached out to Senator Lester Jackson for help. The two of us met with a city official who was scheduled to retire soon. He didn't seem to care or have any interest in the industrial flooding on Dawes Avenue. His nonchalant attitude led me to contact Otis Johnson, the mayor at the time. He listened to my concerns and agreed to attend our next community meeting. He kept his word and brought an army of city officials with him. Mt. Bethel Missionary Baptist Church, where we hold our monthly meetings, was filled to capacity.

Ordinarily, the community residents don't come out to the neighborhood association meetings, but they showed up for this one. A number of employees from city hall were also there, including the city manager, city aldermen, director of affordable housing, and many other city officials. This was only the first of a few meetings with the city; they continued for several months.

City officials came in numbers, nearly all of them making promises. None of them accomplished anything other than spending a lot of money on a consulting firm from Indiana.

The consultants came to our meetings with questions and suggestions, but I believe the city knew exactly what they were going to do before we even began the process. The city offered the residents a buyout, even though, according to one of the consultants, "It would have been cheaper to correct the drainage problem" than buy out the residents.

Promises from the city officials about the revitalization of Ogeecheeton decreased as the community was kicked to the curb yet again.

Most of the residents in the Dawes community sold their properties to the city. Only two or three residents continued to hold out.

Through it all, I remain hopeful that God will work that situation out. He has brought Ogeecheeton a mighty long way and I am confident that He won't leave us now.

As I look back on my life and all that I have experienced and accomplished, I am especially grateful for my life because it has been 20 years since doctors claimed I had a stroke and I'm still here. To God be the glory, because He's been so good to me. I have a wonderful loving wife who is my best friend and confidante. We've been married for the last 17 years and we will remain married until God calls us home.

We are both retired and raising our 12-year-old grandson, Jalen Gordon, who keeps us on our toes—or, as he puts it, "keeps us young." God has truly blessed us and I will forever be grateful.

Johnnie Mae is director of the senior ministry in our church, and in 2013, we were blessed to visit the Holy Land Experience in Orlando, Florida. This park recreates the architecture and themes of the ancient city of Jerusalem.

In 2014, the senior ministry traveled to Ft. Lauderdale, Florida, where we enjoyed a three-day, two-night trip. We had to charter two buses because there were so many people traveling with us. This mini vacation included a four-hour cruise up millionaire's row, with humorous commentary about the many interesting sights and beautiful homes provided by the captain. When the boat docked, the captain yelled, "All ashore!" and we were directed to the unique dining room, where a delicious dinner of barbeque ribs, chicken, boiled shrimp, and all the trimmings had been prepared. The servers continued to pass the plates again and again until we had truly eaten all we could. After dinner, we were invited to a comedy show, where several people from our group participated.

I've enjoyed visiting a lot of states but I must say that New York is my favorite. My sister-in-law, Regina Prince, her daughter, Annette Nottingham, and my father-in-law, John Prince, all live in the same building on Rutland Road in Brooklyn. We've been going to visit them there every year for the past seven years. When we go, we stay for between two and three weeks at a time.

When he picks us up at the airport, my father-in-law immediately turns over the keys to his Cadillac SUV. As soon as we hit the ground in Brooklyn, the very first thing we do is get a slice of New York pizza. There's nothing like it. Then we head to Pitkin Avenue to get an Italian icy. It's the best icy I've ever had because it's made with real fruit.

Regina has already purchased tickets for us to see either a Broadway or off-Broadway show. We've seen so many plays over the years; I can't recall all the names. We've seen *The Color Purple, Trip to Bountiful, A Streetcar Named Desire, Choir Boy*, and *A Raisin in the Sun* to name just a few. After the show, we head to BBQ's on 42nd Street, our favorite post-theater spot to eat.

Because of my interest in historical sites, I create a new agenda each year, which always includes something new and exciting to visit. One year it was the Abyssinian Baptist Church in Harlem, where Adam Clayton Powell served as pastor. The church was absolutely beautiful, but my day would not have been complete if we hadn't gone to 125th Street to sightsee and eat some good old fish and chips. One year we ate at Sylvia's, a famous soul food restaurant. While I truly enjoyed the soul food at Sylvia's, Johnnie Mac longed for some authentic Chinese food.

Jalen, Johnnie Mae, and Richard

Chinatown is a favorite spot for tourists and locals alike. One year while we were walking through the seafood section of Chinatown, I saw a barrel of frogs for sale. That's right: live jumping frogs! I thought that since frog legs are considered a delicacy, why not buy your own and cook the legs ourselves? It made sense to me.

In Chinatown you can find anything you could ever want to eat or buy. From cologne to designer handbags, they have it all. If you're looking to purchase knockoff items, I promise you'll find them some-where around Chinatown. As soon as you emerge from the subway, you are immediately greeted by people asking, "You want designer bag?" "Wallet?" "Watch?" "Cologne?" "Designer jeans?" "What you need?"

What I wanted to buy was an authentic 14-karat gold chain but they weren't able to help me with that. For that, I needed to see a jeweler, and Canal Street was overflowing with jewelry stores.

We were soon overwhelmed and we realized we needed an experi-enced person to help us on this journey. So we did what we should have done from the start: we called my sister-in-law Regina and she came to our rescue. Regina knew how to wheel and deal. Even though she wasn't able to come right away, she arranged for her close friend and coworker Valencia to meet us. Valencia took us to several jewelers and I found exactly what I was looking for. Because New York City is known for price negotiation, it took me some time to finalize my purchase. I learned quickly that all you had to do was walk away after the vendor gave you a price. Within seconds, they'd be hollering for you to come back so they could offer you a lower price. Some of them even asked me, "What do you want to pay?" This pricing game continues until you reach a price that satisfies you.

One year we were in New York on my wife's birthday and the whole family went to Junior's for dinner to celebrate. Over all, the atmosphere and the food were great, especially the famous cheesecake! It was a bit pricey but I reasoned that nothing is too expensive when it comes to my baby.

A few years ago I noticed that Harlem was changing. This neighborhood that had been predominately black had experienced an increase of white residents walking around the neighborhood. It reminded me of what was happening back home in Savannah. Dilapidated buildings in communities where blacks once resided had been sold to whites for next to nothing. A short while later, the community's ethnic population began to change. As soon as whites moved from the inner city to the suburbs and blacks followed them to these residential communities, the whites leave and return to the city. Most of the time they're moving back to the same community they originally left. Then when they get there, they buy inexpensive buildings, fix them up, and increase property values until the original black residents can't afford to live there anymore. Of course, this kind of gentrification is nothing new; it's been happening for years. Some things will never change.

Vernon Gibson, another friend of Regina's, lives and owns property in Harlem and I'm pretty sure he plans to hold on to it. Vernon is very passionate about antiques and his baseball team, the New York Mets. He is a former volunteer fireman and is known at Citi Field as the New York Mets Fireman Kooler. It was Vernon who, along with Regina, arranged for us to enjoy a professional baseball game. Talk about "Take me out to the ball game!" The game was something that all of us, especially Jalen, will always remember.

You couldn't tell me we weren't VIPs as we entered the main entrance to Citi Field, which serves as a beautiful tribute to Jackie Robinson. Inside, we had seats in the first row to watch the game. A photographer noticed Jalen's Mets jersey and asked if he could videotape it. We said yes and shortly thereafter, Jalen appeared on the Jumbotron at the stadium!

Regina, Vernon, Jalen, Johnnie Mae, and Richard at Citi Field

One of the things that was near the top of my list was a visit to the Schomburg Center for Research in Black Culture, which is located in Harlem. It is one of the leading institutions focusing exclusively on African American, African Diaspora, and African experiences. I wanted to go because I have a collection of large framed photos of various Freedom Fund dinners, including photographs from as far back as 1957 and 1958 that were taken at the Roosevelt Hotel. Pictured are prominent people such as Joe Louis, Jackie Robinson, Adam Clayton Powell, and A. Philip Randolph, among others. Something in my spirit told me to preserve those photos. That's just what I did, and then I had them framed professionally. They look wonderful and I've even loaned them out for display during Black History Month in February.

The highlight of last year's vacation was an event at the Brooklyn Museum. The Sackler Center First Awards honor women who are first in their fields. Anita F. Hill was honored for speaking truth to power. Hill was the subject of Freida Lee Mock's documentary *Anita*, which premiered at the Sundance Film Festival in January of 2013. The documentary depicted Hill's life and all she endured as she tried to speak the truth during the hearing confirmation of Supreme Court Justice Clarence Thomas about the sexual harassment she had faced under Thomas. At the end of documentary, Johnnie Mae and I approached the stage hoping to meet Ms. Hill.

As God would have it, we spoke to her and took photos with her. Johnnie Mae casually mentioned that we were from Savannah and she gave us a huge smile as she said, "I'm sure you all know the story," referring to the situation with Supreme Court Justice Clarence Thomas, who hails from Savannah.

Richard, Anita Hill, & Johnnie Mae

COMMISSIONERS OF CHATHAM COUNTY

CHATHAM COUNTY COURTHOUSE ▬▬▬▬▬▬▬▬▬▬▬▬▬▬▬ http://www.chathamcounty.org
124 BULL STREET
P. O. BOX 8161
SAVANNAH, GEORGIA 31412

(912) 652-7869 VOICE
(912) 652-7874 FAX

PETE LIAKAKIS
Chairman

PRISCILLA D. THOMAS
District 8
Vice Chairman

DEAN KICKLIGHTER
District 7
Chairman Pro Tem

HELEN L. STONE
District 1

JAMES J. HOLMES
District 2

PATRICK SHAY
District 3

PATRICK K. FARRELL
District 4

HARRIS ODELL, JR.
District 5

DAVID M. GELLATLY
District 6

R. E. ABOLT
County Manager

R. JONATHAN HART
County Attorney

SYBIL E. TILLMAN
County Clerk

April 1, 2010

Mr. Richard Law
2901 Pate Street
Savannah, Georgia 31405

Dear Richard:

Thank you for the opportunity to commit to writing my appreciation for what you have done for Chatham County and your community over the several years that we've known each other. You have impressed me with your genuine concern for the welfare of citizens within your neighborhood. Your quiet presence is a testimony to the tenacity of your advocacy for others in their time of need. It is a pleasure to know you.

Further, I would be remiss not to express thank you to your wife who was so kind to me when she worked at the post office on Eisenhower Drive. Thanks to both of you for making Chatham County a better place in which to live.

R. E. Abolt

REA:fqr

CHAPTER 16

City of Savannah - City Council

Van R. Johnson, II
Alderman, District 1
Mayor Pro-Tem

Something happened one day on the road to Damascus that changed the life of a man formerly known as Saul, that changed the trajectory of history and created the greatest apostle who has ever lived, Paul. This dramatic conversion on this ordinary road was the beginning of an incredible journey.

Such is the case of Minister Richard Law, who had a similar experience, not on a Damascus road, but somewhere on the highway between Chatham County, GA and Toombs County, GA, on the road between incarceration and freedom, on the dirt path between the Jim Crow South and equality for all.

As the Apostle Paul used his conversion experience to become a powerful advocate for God, Minister Law has used his conversion experience to not only become God's ambassador, but to become a strong voice against racism

Minister Law can speak from the perspective of a jail cell, because he has been there. Minister Law can speak from the perspective of failed relationships because he has been there. Minister Law can speak from the perspective of someone who has been afflicted by illness because he has been there. Minister Law can speak from the experience of someone who has met racism because he has been there. Most importantly, Minister Richard Law can speak from the perspective of someone who has experienced God's love, redemption, restoration and grace - because he IS there.

Van R. Johnson, II
Mayor Pro Tem
Alderman, District 1
Savannah, GA City Council

Ogeecheeton finally got the new welcome sign! Special thanks to Alderman Van Johnson, City Manager, Stephanie Cutter, and everyone who helped to make this happen. Pictured left to right: Chatham County Chairman Al Scott, Richard Law, Sr., Johnnie M. Law, Senator Lester Jackson, and Alderman Van Johnson.

As I express the goodness of God, I do so only to glorify Him. God has truly been good to me and I can't afford to hold my peace. I did not write my story in hopes of solving racism but rather to share my experience with those who may be experiencing situations similar to that which I endured. It is my prayer that if this memoir is able to help just one person, my life would not be in vain. I want to tell the world that when you are faced with a disabling condition while working on a job, you are entitled to compensation, particularly if your employer caused your condition.

My stroke was brought on by the hatred and racism I endured while employed by Toombs County for over ten years. I was told I would not experience retaliation because I filed an EEO complaint, but that was an outright lie. I was misinformed and I had an attorney who left me hanging. For many years, I felt hurt and betrayed but through God's grace and mercy and by telling my story, I am healing daily. I was hurt by so many people while I lived in Toombs County. But God turned around the evil I endured and it helped me to grow.

Some of those same folk were not as fortunate because most of them are now deceased or have difficulties with their health. This reminds me of God's word concerning the treatment of others: "You reap whatever you sow." An important lesson is to always treat others as you want to be treated. As for me, I've learned to be humble while putting others before myself.

There were times in my life when I'd walk to a nursing home or a hospital just to visit the sick. As I walked, many people drove past while others stopped to offer me a ride. I never accepted because at that time I didn't trust anyone. The pain and suffering I experienced from Toombs County had damaged my inner soul and I felt that I needed solitude. I know people wondered why I was walking and I'm sure many of them reached their own conclusions, but they never heard my story.

I truly believe that everything the devil stole from me God has given it back and more. What happened to me in Toombs County caused a sickness that nearly ended my life, but through it all, I continued to hold on to that blood-stained banner. I've endured many painful and traumatic events in my life, but I am confident that these experiences caused me to change my life. I was able to grow and become the man God would have me be. I am no longer an alcoholic or a drug addict. I am not a whoremonger but a devoted husband who adores and loves his wife. God has blessed me with a wonderful woman and I truly love her with all my heart. Not a day goes by that I don't remind her of my love.

Some of my family members and friends have joked that I've got it going on. Some think I'm well off, but they don't know my story and all that I've had to endure. You see, I am the son of a King and an heir to His throne. He is rich and that makes me rich.

I've learned many things through all my trials and tribulations but a few stand out more than others. First and foremost, I've learned to love and honor God. His word reminds me that He is a jealous God and we should put no one before Him. I read the Bible because it is the source of everything I need to know, especially when I need to be comforted or when someone else needs what comfort I can offer. My ministry is for the glorification of God alone. My ministry has allowed me to touch hearts and souls wherever I am.

I read God's word religiously and I've learned to pray before reading so that He will make it all very clear to me. Any problems I face, His word gives me the answer. I've learned to fast and pray, to wait, and to believe. I've learned to never give up on Him. I know that what He's done for others, He is able to do for me. God has delivered me from a world of darkness and He has brought me into His marvelous light. I'm walking and talking with my Creator and my Prince of Peace. I claim victory over anyone or anything that is a hindrance to my life. I know without a shadow of a doubt that I am the child of a King.

I am so thankful to God that He spared my life so that I might tell my story. My God is an awesome God, and right now and every day I lift my hands in adoration and say, "I thank you, Lord!"

I believe that we as people are striving to eliminate racism from our lives, but there are demonic spirits in this world whose main focus is to destroy and kill. That's always been our major problem. Looking back at the civil rights movement of the 1950s and Dr. Martin Luther King, Jr.'s, legacy, I know we've come a long way and many things have changed. However, we still have a long way to go. Laws are made to ensure the rights of people but laws are often made to be broken. Everyone knows it is a human right to be treated equally but people still disregard the law. I continue to say there are two sets of laws in this world, one set for blacks and another for whites. I know that if I had been a white man when I suffered a stroke, things would have been very different for me. It is unfortunate to say, but there is still a great deal of racism that exists today.

Everywhere you turn, you'll see racism. Can we change? Can we stop racism for good? Some things will never change. But I do believe that while we have a long way to go, we cannot give up the fight. If we stop fighting to end racism—if we stop striving to ensure equal rights for all—where will we be? Some things may never change, but we must keep trying. I believe that God will see us through, just as He did with me.

RICHARD LAW, SR. was born in Savannah, Georgia where he still lives today with his wife Johnnie Mae Law. Between them, they have five children and seven grandchildren.

Richard graduated from Alfred E. Beach High School in 1971 before attending Savannah Technical College and Armstrong State College.

For many years, Richard was employed by International Paper and Toombs County until he was disabled in 1994.

Faced with personal struggles of drugs, alcohol, and women, Richard's life was transformed when he became a born-again Christian. In 2000, Richard joined the St. Paul CME Church and in 2003 he became a licensed minister. Richard's love for people is evident in his visits to hospitals, nursing homes, and the jail.

Presently, Richard is president of the Ogeecheeton-Dawes Neighborhood Association. He is a past member of Savannah Historic District Board of Review. He is past Vice President of the Hungry Club and past member of the EOA Policy Council. And he is an active member of the St. Paul CME Church and the Senior Citizen Ministry.